GROSS
AMERICA

GROSS AMERICA

Your Coast-to-Coast Guide to All Things Gross

Richard Faulk

JEREMY P. TARCHER/PENGUIN

a member of Penguin Group (USA) Inc.

New York

JEREMY P. TARCHER/PENGUIN
Published by the Penguin Group
Penguin Group (USA) Inc., 375 Hudson Street, New York, New York
10014, USA • Penguin Group (Canada), 90 Eglinton Avenue East, Suite 700,
Toronto, Ontario M4P 2Y3, Canada (a division of Pearson Penguin Canada Inc.) • Penguin
Books Ltd, 80 Strand, London WC2R 0RL, England • Penguin Ireland, 25 St Stephen's Green,
Dublin 2, Ireland (a division of Penguin Books Ltd) • Penguin Group (Australia),
250 Camberwell Road, Camberwell, Victoria 3124, Australia (a division of Pearson Australia
Group Pty Ltd) • Penguin Books India Pvt Ltd, 11 Community Centre, Panchsheel Park,
New Delhi–110 017, India • Penguin Group (NZ), 67 Apollo Drive, Rosedale, North Shore
0632, New Zealand (a division of Pearson New Zealand Ltd) • Penguin Books
(South Africa) (Pty) Ltd, 24 Sturdee Avenue, Rosebank, Johannesburg 2196, South Africa

Penguin Books Ltd, Registered Offices: 80 Strand, London WC2R 0RL, England

Library of Congress Cataloging-in-Publication Data

Faulk, Richard.
Gross America: your coast-to-coast guide to all things gross / by Richard Faulk.
p.   cm.
Includes index.
ISBN 978-1-58542-941-7
1. Curiosities and wonders—United States—Guidebooks.   2. Eccentrics and eccentricities—
United States—Guidebooks.   I. Title.
E158.F38   2012   2012026782
032.02—dc23

BOOK DESIGN BY NICOLE LAROCHE

Neither the publisher nor the author is engaged in rendering professional advice or services to
the individual reader. The ideas, procedures, and suggestions contained in this book are not
intended as a substitute for consulting with your physician. All matters regarding your health
require medical supervision. Neither the author nor the publisher shall be liable or responsible
for any loss or damage allegedly arising from any information or suggestion in this book.

While the author has made every effort to provide accurate telephone numbers, Internet addresses,
and other contact information at the time of publication, neither the publisher nor the author
assumes any responsibility for errors, or for changes that occur after publication. Further,
the publisher does not have any control over and does not assume any responsibility
for author or third-party websites or their content.

ALWAYS LEARNING   PEARSON

Contents

THE NORTHEAST

THE FAR WEST:
Noncontiguous States

Introduction

Welcome to you, the reader, whether you are already committed to this grisly transcontinental adventure or merely testing the murky waters with a nervous toe tip.

If it is unadulterated gross you are looking for, I invite you to plunge right in. The articles are self-contained and mostly speak for themselves, so you can jump the tour and strike out on your own whenever you like. If you are looking for suggestions, I might direct you to the so-called *sperm tree* of Los Angeles. That's pretty rank. Or maybe *flameless cremation* in Florida—that's ghastly also, no two ways about it.

If you are a more methodical traveler, however, you might prefer to glance at the itinerary first. As befits our journey into the bizarre, we begin in the West and make our way across the country against the course of the sun, *widdershins*, as the witches used to say. Along the way, I will point out places of note that are as strange and varied as the nation itself.

Our stops include respectable, highbrow places, like universities, public museums, and professional archives; but we will also peek into the peculiar collections of enthusiastic amateurs. We will ogle strange animals and plant life, gaze from wild vistas, and take a bench at a local festival or two for a taste of some down-home weirdness. Any place might be a secret repository of grossological interest.

In this book you will find nothing resembling a plot. However, there are connections that emerge from time to time. Read long enough, and you are certain to start recognizing certain recurring names and concepts. I have **bolded** some of these and, at the end of each entry, listed references to other places in the book where they appear, so that the curious may follow up. It is therefore equally possible to take this tour geographically or thematically.

One caveat, before I send you on your way. Since there is more than a little science talk in these pages, I should be up-front and tell you that I am not a scientist. Comparative literature is my field, which means that I was trained to do many things in the humanities, and to do them all equally badly. But if there was one thing I learned from my dalliance with the Muses, that is to ask questions and to find ways of answering them. And what is that, if not the first stirring of scientific thought?

If any of the questions I raise in these pages lead you to search for answers of your own, then I shall feel that my dilettantish turn as a natural historian has been amply rewarded—even in those (assuredly very rare) instances when the answers you find suggest that mine are wrong.

Snap Revell at the 11th Annual
Sopchoppy Worm Gruntin' Festival

THE WEST

California

Anything Chocolate-Dipped Is Good . . . ?

WHAT: Hotlix insect candy

WHERE: Pismo Beach

Orange worm, grape cricket, chocolate scorpion, spiced larva . . . no, it's not a recipe for witch's party mix. It's a selection of menu items available from Hotlix, a Southern California–based confectioner that specializes in candy-coated insects.

Originally known for its fiery, cinnamon-saturated Toothpix, the company entered almost unwittingly into entomo-gastronomy in 1982 when it concocted a tequila-flavored lollipop with a worm center. The insect was just an afterthought, a flourish to evoke the iconic worm at the bottom of a mezcal bottle.

(For those who have better things to do than keep track of Mexican spirits, it is in mezcal, not tequila, where you will find the worm. Both liquors are distilled from the spiky agave plant, but tequila is a more regulated appellation. Tequila, the champagne to mezcal's sparkling wine, would *never* stoop to such a vulgarity. Not a major distinction, but the cognoscenti and *borrachos* care.)

The simple addition of a worm was as fortuitous for Hotlix as it was for the Mexican liquor industry. The success of the worm lolly begat the company's cricket sucker, the bug-laden "amber" brittle, edible miniature ant farms, and even the savory snack mix Larvets—crunchy worms, available in cheddar cheese, BBQ, and "Mexican spice" flavors.

Potential customers can take comfort in the fact that they will not be eating mere garden-variety insects. All of Hotlix's bugs are raised specifically for human consumption and are fed a special diet of oatmeal, apple and banana peels, and other wholesome delicacies. Every week more than 50,000 crickets alone are harvested to keep the snack shelves stocked.

The most daunting Hotlix offering is perhaps the chocolate-dipped scorpion. Although the stinger is apparently no longer venomous once the arthropod is dead, it is removed for good measure prior to the scorpion's posthumous chocolate plunge. There are no reports confirming whether or not it tastes like chicken.

If you can't make it to Pismo Beach, Hotlix are available in candy and novelty stores across the country and can be ordered directly from the Hotlix website: **www.hotlix.biz**.

Attack of the Fungus-Zombie Ants

WHAT: Megaloponera foetens: The stink ant of the Cameroon

WHERE: The Museum of Jurassic Technology, Culver City

Venice Boulevard starts at the western edge of the continent. Rising out of the eccentric coastal town of Venice Beach (forever hallowed for its appearance in the roller-disco masterpiece *Xanadu*), the road arcs northeast, like an arrow from a bow, cutting deep into the heart of the sprawling urban expanse of greater Los Angeles, until its path starts to falter and wobble southward and then vanishes somewhere downtown.

Shortly before it begins its descent, Venice Boulevard passes through a palimpsest cityscape where '90s strip malls and In-N-Out Burgers have not quite overwritten blocks of cheap ethnic eateries praised by prowling foodies, and old stucco shops, whose painted signs advertise services like floor installation and karate instruction. This is Culver City.

Amid this jumble of old and not-so-old, sharing a block with an auto body shop, you will find an incongruous building whose colorful fresco walls and narrow marble fountain, choked with reeds, would seem more at home on the shores of the Mediterranean than in a shabby Southern California suburb. This is the Museum of Jurassic Technology.

Established in 1988 by artist and industrial filmmaker David Hildebrand Wilson and his wife Diana Drake Wilson, the Museum of Jurassic Technology, which purports to document life in the unexplained "Lower Jurassic," is arguably less a museum than a wry piece of performance art whose bizarre exhibits challenge visitors' faith in scientific authority even as they incite an awe-like appreciation for the miraculously weird world we live in.

The museum's eclectic—even downright daffy—holdings include miniature artworks carved in fruit pits, etched human hairs, and set into the eye of sewing needles; exhibits of decaying midcentury dice from the collection of actor and professional prestidigitator Ricky Jay; displays of little-known folk remedies; pages of insane, rambling letters written to the astronomers at

Mount Wilson Observatory; and an account of a hunt for an improbable animal called the *Deprong Mori*. And these are just the easier-to-talk-about exhibits.

Blithely thwarting our expectations of a modern museum, the Museum of Jurassic Technology more closely resembles that institution's direct ancestor, the Renaissance **cabinet of curiosities**. With its refusal to distinguish art from science and an uncanny ability to construct a mood of hushed surreality, the museum playfully evokes how it must have felt to enter those antique chambers where the learned and wealthy used to display their collections of marvelous and unexpected objects acquired from all corners of a world that had suddenly been vastly expanded. Indeed, the faintly euphemistic noun *curiosity* does not do justice to the experience. Better to use the German term: *Wunderkammer,* or *wonder room.*

The wondrous assemblage of oddities at the MJT strains credulity, and the exhibit descriptions, at once florid and opaque, obscure as much as they explain. Everything about the museum instills a sense of doubt. And the deadpan demeanor of proprietor David Wilson does nothing to allay your suspicion that somewhere a joke is being played—even if you can never quite pinpoint what it is.

"Life in all of its manifold and perplexing beauty . . ." – from the Megaloponera foetens exhibit

One of the museum's more celebrated—and without doubt its most horrific—exhibits is on *Megaloponera foetens*, or the "stink ant of the Cameroon of West Central Africa."

A sign at the bottom of the display recounts at length the story of a fungus that over countless millennia has evolved in tandem with a species of large African ant. Spores of the *Tomentella* that are inhaled by the stink ant cause erratic behavior in their host. Suddenly turned maverick, the afflicted ant will strike out from its colony on the forest floor and begin to climb the jungle under-growth. As if directed by a sinister intelligence, the purposeful insect stops its ascent at a precise height and grabs hold of the foliage with its mandibles. Then, it waits. In due course, gestat-ing spores will burst out from the host's head, producing a large fungal spike that, once sufficiently nourished from the corpse of the unhappy stink ant, will rain new spores down on the colony below, thus starting the reproductive cycle anew.

And sure enough, in the case is a large ant whose head is im-paled to a snaky tropical vine by a large, fungal spike.

As incredible as it sounds, the story is substantially correct. But there are holes in it: *Megaloponera foetens* is an improper variant of *Megaponera foetens*. And *Megaponera foetens* is more known for organizing hunts against termites than for falling prey to toxic spores. *Camponotus leonardi*, the carpenter ant, is the more usual victim of spore-induced zombiefication. As for the *Tomentella* fungus, that is completely wrong. The species in question is *Ophiocordyceps unilateralis*, and it has been torment-ing ants for almost 50 million years . . . in South America, South-east Asia, and *southern*—not west-central—Africa. Strange holes, these. Holes, which, after pondering them at length, one almost starts to wonder might not be simple error or carelessness, but perverse—almost *willfully* misleading—holes.

Even in the so-called Information Age, it is very difficult to fact-check the exhibits at the Museum of Jurassic Technology, with their elusive blending of fact and fancy. But once you find yourself searching through piles of academic articles on the tax-onomy and various pathologies of hymenopteran, you begin to feel that you have somehow played into the museum's hands. While the satisfaction of visiting a conventional museum lies to a degree in the joy of effortless enlightenment, as if one had been handed the CliffsNotes to one facet of the universe, the effect of the MJT is to leave feeling less certain and more ignorant than when you came in. But ignorance is power—or rather the *awareness* of one's own ignorance is. For it's in coming to grips with how little we know that wisdom is born. That's the message Socrates died for daring to teach, and it's the humbling jolt that the MJT gleefully delivers.

Trust nothing, but be ready to believe anything could be the motto of this perplexing museum. For an institution that is sometimes dismissed as trading in hipster irony, it is a disarmingly direct and powerful piece of practical wisdom.

The Museum of Jurassic Technology is open Thursday through Sunday. The suggested donation is $5. Learn more at **mjt.org**.

See also:

Cabinets of curiosity: Ward's Natural Science Establishment, New York

Two-Fisted Fishing

WHAT: The annual Grunion Run

WHERE: Cabrillo Marine Aquarium, San Pedro

The coast of southern California is home to a unique type of fishing that requires no boats, no rods, and no hooks. The only equipment needed is your own two hands.

Late at night throughout the summer months, beaches from

Santa Barbara to Baja California are crawling with a small, sardine-like fish called the *grunion*. This most unusual fish leaves the ocean to lay its eggs on land. It does this by waiting until the tide is at its highest and then riding the waves far up the shore. Once the beached grunion has squirmed away to a point where the waves won't disturb its work, it digs a hole and deposits its eggs in the wet sand.

A grunion in its natural habitat

Meanwhile, would-be grunion hunters lie in wait under cover of darkness. On a good night, the beach will be covered with thousands of these slender, squiggling fish, flashing silver in the moonlight. The hunters switch on their flashlights and scoop up handfuls of muddy grunions. This can be a frustrating way to fish, because the slick grunions have a tendency to squirm through fingers and flop back to the safety of the waves, but in California the only legal way to catch this fish is with your bare hands.

Grunions breed from March through August. The nights nearest the full and new moon, when the tide is highest and fish come out in greatest numbers to lay their eggs, are called Grunion Runs.

The Cabrillo Aquarium, located just south of Los Angeles, hosts an annual Grunion Run event, with trained guides to explain the strange breeding habits of the fish. While you can eat the grunions you catch (they have a strong flavor, like mackerel), the aquarium guides prefer that you release the grunions back into the ocean so they live to run another day.

Find out when the next Grunion Run is on by visiting the Cabrillo Aquarium's website: **www.cabrillomarineaquarium.org**.

Vampire Redwoods

WHAT: Redwood albinism

WHERE: Henry Cowell Redwoods State Park, Felton

An albino redwood

California's redwood country is a narrow strip of land that starts at Monterey Bay, two hours south of San Francisco, and continues up the Pacific Coast into Oregon. Beneath the shadows of the majestic *Sequoia sempervirens* unfolds a mysterious twilight world, home to a ragtag assortment of hippies, survivalists, anarchists, and idealists who have turned their backs on the workaday world and opted to live somewhere out of time.

Perhaps the redwoods' most famous denizen is the elusive anthropoid Bigfoot. But for more than one hundred and fifty years, rumors have circulated of another cryptozoological specimen: ghostly redwoods with waxy, colorless leaves and weak, brittle trunks. Parasitically feeding off older trees, and dying back in dry weather only to spectrally rematerialize during the rains, these stunted "everwhites" have been called the vampires of the plant kingdom.

Biologists, however, call them *albino redwoods*.

Albinism in redwoods is an exceedingly rare mutation. Fewer than thirty specimens are known to exist, and eight of them are at the Cowell State Park in the hilly forest between Santa Cruz and the Silicon Valley. Their exact location, though, is a secret closely kept by biologists and rangers who study the fragile trees and wish to keep them safe from the clumsy tread of the idly curious.

Albinism (from the Latin word for *white*) is a genetic disorder that prevents a body from producing melanin, the pigment that gives color to our skin, hair, and eyes. Since melanin's primary job is to protect living creatures from ultraviolet rays, albinos are prone to sunburn and skin cancer. Melanin deficiency can affect eyesight as well. But, on the scale of genetic variations, albinism in people and domestic animals is a reasonably benign mutation.

Among animals in the wild, it's a different story. An albino's bright white hide acts as a warning to prey and a target for predators, pretty much guaranteeing a short tenure among the living.

But albinism in plants is an outright death sentence. Without pigment, there is no chlorophyll; without chlorophyll, there is no photosynthesis; and without photosynthesis, a plant cannot eat. It's hard to see how an albino plant can even start living in the first place.

It is the redwood's peculiar form of reproduction that allows albinos of this species to have a shot at survival. Redwoods can grow from seeds, like other trees, but they also have the option of reproducing asexually by sending out shoots from wherever they like—root, stump, or even fallen branch. Albino redwoods are able to grow because they can remain grafted to their parent tree, which they tap for nourishment.

Biologists do not yet fully understand the mechanics of that process. And that's just one of the riddles of redwoods that scientists are working to solve. It turns out that these mighty trees are surprisingly tough nuts to crack.

Genetically speaking, redwoods are *hexaploid*, which means that every one of their cells has six sets of chromosomes. Human beings, on the other hand, like almost all other animals, are mere diploids, who have only two sets of chromosomes (one inherited from Mom, the other from Dad). While we humans have a total of 46 chromosomes in each cell, redwood trees have 66.

Every time a cell divides, its DNA splits too. Each time that happens, there is a tiny chance that there will be a mistake in duplicating the DNA. These mistakes are what we call *mutations*. More sets of chromosomes means that there are not only more possible genetic combinations in redwoods, but also more possibilities for mutations.

For many of us, the word *mutation* conjures images of X-Men or giant, irradiated insects. But for scientists, mutation means something much humbler—just an accidental genetic variant. Most mutations do nothing to improve an organism's odds of survival. And many are downright harmful, like albinism. But a minuscule percentage of mutations are design improvements to the species. The redwood's large number of chromosomes provides many opportunities for mutation, which in turn allows them to be highly inventive in their survival strategies and rapidly adaptive to their environment. It also makes their genetics vastly more complex than ours and presents researchers with a statistical nightmare.

For a plant that should not actually exist, albino redwoods

do quite well for themselves. Vulnerable to climate fluctuations, they nevertheless spring back eagerly when conditions are favorable. If the good weather holds they can grow to a respectable 70 feet tall off their parent tree's largess (although 70 feet is relatively stumpy for a species that typically maxes out nearer 400 feet).

Taller and longer-lived than their arboreal peers, redwoods are sometimes called *the kings of the forest*. But if we review the history of our human royal houses, we might reconsider that it is actually the redwood's albino scions—the pallid, pampered, and ineffectual little dauphins that somehow manage to survive, and even thrive, on the backs of their more illustrious ancestors— that might better deserve the title of nature's aristocrats.

The Necropolis by the Bay

WHAT: The seventeen cemeteries of Colma

WHERE: Colma, California

There comes a point in the life of every major city when death becomes a serious managerial problem.

The dead don't use any resources, and they don't take up much space individually. But they don't go anywhere either, and their number is continually increasing. Inevitably the real estate needs of a city's living citizens start to conflict with the claims of its dead, and something's got to give.

In San Francisco at the turn of the nineteenth century, that crisis hit suddenly, and it called for a drastic solution.

When the City by the Bay was established in 1776, it was little more than a lonesome Spanish fort at the tip of a long peninsula at the edge of the world. The burial needs of the fifty-odd soldiers stationed there were amply met by the single graveyard at nearby Mission Dolores. And so it went, even after the Spanish left and the old fort blossomed into a frontier town. But when gold was discovered near Sacramento in 1848, the port of San Francisco suddenly found itself the entryway for a mighty stream of gold-struck immigrants from all points of the globe. From the end of 1848 to the end of 1849, San Francisco's population exploded from fewer than a thousand to 25,000. By 1870, it had matured into a respectable city of 150,000 souls.

Through disease and fire and the general lawlessness of the Barbary Coast, the population of San Francisco's dead boomed right along with that of the living. Twenty-five new cemeteries had been constructed since the early days and they were all perilously full.

By 1880, the city was running out of space. Land was so expensive that expansion was out of the question for the city's cemeteries. Indeed, it was the city itself that was considering moving into the cemeteries, as developers began to regard these hallowed resting places as woefully underutilized plots of urban real estate. Meanwhile, the public, which was just becoming aware of a new scientific discovery called **germs**, wanted all those filthy corpses out of their backyard. Citizens indignant and horrified that the microbial exhalations from "half a million pounds of putridity"—as one newspaper editorial would characterize the city's dead that were interred each year—should be allowed to "rise to the surface from the deepest grave to poison both the earth and air," right there in the middle of town!

The city council was forced to take action. In 1900, San Francisco closed its cemeteries and forbade new interment within the city limits. In 1914, it took the next logical step and banished the dead altogether—no more would they remain selfish squatters on fallow urban land or pollute the air with their deathly miasma. They were to be exhumed and transferred. Officially, they would become someone else's problem.

Cemetery City

That someone else was Colma, a swath of unincorporated land just to the south of San Francisco. Lightly populated and easy to reach by horse, streetcar, or train, Colma was also happy to take on the dead from its northern neighbor.

The community had, in fact, entered the funeral game well before San Francisco closed its cemeteries. But the city's restrictions were a boon to Colma's burgeoning post-life service industry.

Hundreds of thousands of bodies were deported from San Francisco in a diaspora of the dead. Fancy people sent their loved ones across the bay to Oakland's Mountain View Cemetery, a particularly lovely site designed by Central Park's architect, Frederick Law Olmsted. But most folk ended up in Colma—including the paupers who had no one to pay the $10 transferal fee and ended up in mass graves.

As the relocation windfall passed, Colma had to get serious about its burial business. Part of its plan was to incorporate as a town, which it did in 1924 under the appropriately cemeterial name *Lawndale*. The name was already taken, but new Lawndale had such a tiny population that seventeen years passed before the Post Office noticed the duplication. In 1941, the town returned to its pre-incorporation designation, *Colma*.

Today, Colma's official stance is an ironic acceptance of its role as San Francisco's necropolis. Its official motto is *It's great to be alive in Colma!* Although in a community where the dead outnumber the living a thousand to one, that might come across as a jibe at a very weighty constituency.

The Colma Historical Association offers cemetery tours by appointment. They'll be happy to show you the final resting place of Wyatt Earp, Joe DiMaggio, Levi Strauss, and other famous Americans who now call Colma home.

Plan your Colma visit at **www.colmahistory.org**.

See also:
Germs: Fecal transplantation therapy, Minnesota

The Hills Have Legs

WHAT: The Tarantula Trek

WHERE: Mt. Diablo, California

Once a year, this Bay Area mountain about 20 miles east of Berkeley earns its sinister name. Every Halloween season the golden slopes of Mt. Diablo shudder beneath the surreptitious step of innumerable sets of furry, spindly spider legs: those of tarantulas emerging from their subterranean burrows, like the undead rising from the grave. But these happy hunters are more likely to be up to monkey business than doing the devil's work.

Spring may turn a young man's fancy toward thoughts of love; but for tarantulas, the season for romance is autumn. When California's Indian summer starts to wane, the latest batch of mature males feel the call of nature. They lose interest in eating and start to burn with a hitherto unknown sense of wanderlust that will compel them to undertake a voyage of sexual discovery from which none will return.

Lovers Not Fighters

Biologically speaking, tarantulas are the world's largest spiders; ethically, they are even bigger chickens—particularly the timid *Aphonopelma smithi* species found on Mt. Diablo. Aside from mating season, it is very rare to see these tarantulas in the wild. Gifted with poor eyesight, their outsized bodies as conspicuous to predators as they are to us, *A. smithi* is not suited for surface living. They prefer to stay in subterranean nests, from whence they pounce, ambush-style, on crickets, birds, and other small prey that stray within striking distance of their front door.

If threatened, *A. smithi* will rear menacingly and extend its fangs. But this is a ruse. While the foe is sizing up the front, the wily tarantula uses its back legs to rub the prickly hairs off its abdomen, which it tosses like miniature javelins right in its attacker's face—*sucka!* The surprise and irritation of these stinging, or *urticating*, hairs give the spider time to take it on the lam.

It is said that the bite of *A. smithi* is about as painful and dangerous as a bee sting. Not that many people know from experience. If you pick up one of these delicate tarantulas, it is more likely to accidentally snap off one or two of its own legs in a frenzied struggle to escape than it is to bite you. So if you see one in the wild, let it be—not for your sake, but for the poor spider's.

What is it, then, that can drive these reluctant beasts out of the safety of their lairs? From what direction emanates the inescapable force that can lure these superterranean misfits out into the dangerous open? *Cherchez la femme,* of course.

The Secret Vice of Tarantulas

Lady tarantulas spend their lives entirely underground—and a long life it is, too: generally twenty, even up to forty years. It is the males whom nature deems expendable. It takes a male tarantula seven years to reach sexual maturity. Once he does, his only purpose is to "go over the top," like a First World War soldier scrambling out of the trenches, to brave a no-man's-land of predators and hostile terrain, and deliver his sperm to as many female tarantulas as he can before his imminent and inevitable death.

And that's not even the lurid part.

When the male *A. smithi* first feels that itch in the loins, he spins a silken mattress which will serve as conjugal bed for himself—and himself alone. His litter-strewn bachelor's den now transformed into a louche masturbatorium, Mr. *Smithi* settles down upon his wanking web, and, in one fell swoop, releases seven long years of celibate living.

Once the deed has been done, *A. smithi* scoops up his spidery seed in a pair of appendages near his face called *pedipalps*, which are something between a jaw and a claw. When he finds a receptive female, he will seize her fangs to prevent her from eating him and then use his face to deposit some of the sperm from his pedipalps onto her lower abdomen.

It doesn't sound like much fun, but male tarantulas will do this over and over again in a series of hit-and-run hookups that ends only when the male is killed by a predator, devoured by a ravenous mate (happily, this is rare), or simply drops dead from hunger.

Now that you know the seedy backstory, if you care to actually observe these love-crazed giant spiders in their natural habitat, Mt. Diablo hosts Tarantula Treks every year from mid-

October to mid-November. For three hours from sunset to night-fall, park rangers lead visitors on a gentle two-and-a-half-mile walk to search out these doomed, eight-legged lovers. Be sure to reserve your spot early, because the tours fill up quickly. For some reason, people seem to regard this orgy of sex and death as good family fun.

Reserve your spot on the next Tarantula Trek at **www** .mdia.org.

You Can Get a Monument for *What?*

WHAT: Pioneer Monument

WHERE: Donner Memorial State Park, Truckee

The Donner Party Statue

In a clearing in the pines of a California state park stands a grand monument, 20 feet tall at the base and topped with a supersized pioneer family cast in bronze: Ma, bent beneath the protective arm of her husband; Pa, shielding his eyes as he peers westward into a bold new future; the Young 'Uns, crouching behind, timid and uncertain yet drawn inexorably toward the fate that beckons. Dedicated in 1918, the Pioneer Monument was erected to commemorate the hardy folk who followed the Emi-grant Trail to populate the American West.

In particular, though, it memorializes one band of settlers, whose unimaginable hardships have shaped our collective nightmares for a century and a half.

"Never take no cutoffs and hurry along as fast as you can."–12-year-old Virginia Reed, Donner Party survivor

During the great frontier era of the mid-1800s, more than half a million pioneers forsook their homes in the East, braving desert heat, frozen mountain passes, Indian attacks, disease, and privation for the chance to start a new life in Oregon and California.

As far as we know, fewer than two dozen of them were cannibals.

But, in California's mountainous Lake Tahoe region, one-time gateway to the Pacific, it is impossible to escape reminders of America's most recognized band of homegrown humanivores, the infamous Donner Party. There is Donner Lake and Donner Park, Donner Pass and Donner Summit. The name *Donner* is thrown against random nouns with such ferocious abandon that it would make even a Smurf blush.

But there is a reason that name is stamped so indelibly in the Tahoe region. The ill-starred Donner Party was a disaster that spectacularly embodied almost everything that could go wrong with a pioneer wagon train. The dystopic flip side to the American Dream, in which every mountain is climbable and every stream can be forded, the catastrophe of the Donner Party immediately captured the nation's lurid imagination. Now it has become ingrained in our history—one singularly horrific incident standing in for the countless unremembered tragedies that played out along the Emigrant Trail.

It is a story that begins in spring 1846, when nine new Conestoga wagons left Springfield, Illinois, headed for the greener pastures of California. It was smooth sailing at first—until party leader Jacob Donner decided to follow an untested "shortcut" across Utah's Great Basin. What should have been a weeklong trek stretched into a monthlong slog. Arriving at the Great Salt Lake short on supplies, demoralized, and woefully behind schedule, the wagon train now had to race for the Sierra Nevada before the autumn snows made the mountain range impassable.

They were one day short.

As the exhausted travelers camped just 1,000 feet below the pass that led down and out of the Sierras, the first snowfall of the season hit, dumping five feet overnight. Soon five feet became twenty, and the eighty-seven men, women, and children of the Donner Party were stranded without food, without fuel, and without hope.

Throughout the course of the harshest winter in memory, search parties from Sutter's Fort on the western side of the mountains would eventually rescue forty-six survivors. But it took many attempts. For those trapped longest in the mountains, the only option was to eat the remains of their dead companions or to perish themselves. As many as twenty-one of them chose to eat.

When the last survivors were reached, more dead than alive and more raving and bestial than human, rescuers also found the partially butchered remains of ten frozen corpses.

The Donner Party memorial stands near the site of one of the cabins that sheltered the snowbound travelers during the dreadful winter of '46. The stone pedestal was built 22 feet tall, the same height as the snow that blocked the pass. A bronze plaque honors the frontier tragedy, but tastefully omits any reference to cannibalism. In another step away from its gruesome past, the monument was later rededicated to the memory of all the pioneers who passed through the Sierras. Similarly, the nearby Donner Party Museum, built in 1927, is now officially the Emigrant Trail Museum.

The Perils of Eating One's Own

If the story of the Donner Party hasn't left a bad taste in your mouth, here is some advice to any would-be cannibals. One: Don't do it! It's gross and morally repugnant. Two: If circumstances do compel you to eat another human being, avoid the brains. Eating them is a good way of catching one of a variety of terrible neurological diseases called *transmissible spongiform encephalopathies*, or *TSEs*. You can catch these diseases (aka *pathies*) by ingesting rogue proteins called *prions* that attack your brain (aka *encephalos*) and leave it riddled with tiny holes like a soggy sponge (aka *spongiform*). While the prions are relentlessly unraveling your brain, you will experience memory loss, hallucinations, physical quirks and seizures, and creeping dementia, all of which will worsen over the months it will take you to finally die from the illness.

And, no, cooking won't prevent TSE contamination, so don't even bother.

If this seems too hideous to be true, consider the story of the Fore (*FORE-ay*) people of Papua New Guinea. In the early twentieth century, the Fore were being decimated by a TSE called *kuru*. Visiting scientists in the 1940s determined that the cause of the epidemic was a funeral practice that required mourners to eat their dearly departed—particularly the brain—as a sign of respect. Somewhere along the line, one of the Fore had inherited the rare genetic defect that causes kuru. When that person died, the condition was passed on to everyone who ate him—and *they* passed it on to everyone who ate *them,* and so on, and so on. The epidemic did not end until the Fore were persuaded to give up cannibalism.

Beware the Zombie Cow

Well, you might be thinking, *that's ancient history.* But don't be so sure: TSEs have hit closer to home. In 1984, the United Kingdom experienced an outbreak of mad cow disease, which in humans causes the TSE *Creutzfeldt-Jakob disease.* The outbreak in cows was contained by the late '90s, but since Creutzfeldt-Jakob incubates very slowly, more cases in humans are still being diagnosed to this day. So far 167 people have died from this event. Since 2003, there have been four reported cases of mad cow disease in the US—including the most recent discovery of an infected California cow in April 2012. In each instance, however, the disease is believe to be contained and there are no known human fatalities.

The initial UK outbreak shocked the world and led to a reevaluation of the way we raise livestock when it was learned that the probable source was tainted animal feed that included ground-up diseased *cow brains.* Oops! Apparently someone confused the peaceable, herbivorous, non-cannibalistic cow with the ravening, brain-eating zombie.

So the lesson abundantly illustrated here is: Don't feed brains to the animals, and never, *never* eat a human brain!

See also:

Cannibalism: The Alferd Packer Memorial Restaurant and Grill, Colorado

Eau De Je Ne Sais Quoi

WHAT: The sperm trees of Los Angeles

WHERE: Elysian Park, Los Angeles

Not every Angeleno is familiar with the term *the sperm trees of L.A.*, but if you ask one about the tree that smells like jism, you're guaranteed to get a gasp of recognition.

The phrase was coined in the mid-'80s in "The Straight Dope," a syndicated advice column, when a Los Angeles reader wrote to ask what the name of those trees were in his neighborhood that smelled unnervingly like semen.

This was one puzzler for which even columnist Cecil Adams, self-proclaimed world's smartest human, could find no decisive answer. The botanists and urologists Adams consulted treated him like a nut, while readers from across the country inundated him with conflicting suggestions.

However fatuous the question might have seemed on its face, it ended up exposing some unexpected facts. The first is that there is not just *one* tree that smells like the ejecta of the virile part, but many. Bradford pear, mimosa tree, several species of privet, and the ostentatiously named *tree of heaven* were all nominated for the title.

Another surprise is that there is widespread disagreement over what semen actually smells like. Some semenological experts insist that it has no intrinsic smell but gets its aroma from each man's particular diet. Others argue that there is a consistent scent, but disagree on exactly what that is, and whether it is pleasant or not.

As we will soon see, one tree was eventually crowned the true *sperm tree of L.A.* But the underlying question—what is it that makes a tree smell like semen?—was never answered.

To pick up that thread and attempt to unravel it ourselves requires taking a closer look at the chemistry of scent.

Smell That Smell . . .

The least tangible of our senses, smell is wildly subjective and maddening to describe. One of the very few constants about smell is that the odors of vomit and of rotting human flesh seem to be universally revolting. Beyond that, all bets are off. Indeed, some of the more sublimely delicious aromas are just a hair's breadth away from utterly disgusting. Aged soft cheeses share chemical properties with dirty socks, bad breath, and farts; truffles smell like pigs in heat (or, at least boy pigs think so), and wine connoisseurs debate qualities such as *barnyard* and *pipi de chat*, otherwise known as "cat piss."

At the chemical level, many organic scents, particularly those of decay—rotting flesh, perspiration, rancid cheese—share one thing in common, the presence of a group of molecules known as *amines*. Strongly basic on the pH scale, amines are derivatives of ammonia, which is itself the composite of a single nitrogen atom bonded to three atoms of hydrogen (NH_3 in chemistry shorthand). Amines differ from ammonia and from one another by substituting one or more of those hydrogen atoms with a chemical compound. The amine *trimethylamine*, for example, is $N(CH_3)_3$, and it is responsible for the characteristic reek of rotting fish; its cousins *cadaverine* and *putrescine* speak for themselves.

This discussion of amines helps us solve for the first unknown in our sperm-tree scent equation: *sperm.*

Like other cells, *spermatozoa*—to give the full name of these squiggly tadpoles of romance—have no odor of their own. It's really *semen* we are talking about here, the protective and nutritional fluid that envelops the sperm. Semen has a complex chemistry that develops as it progresses through the body's obstacle course of urinary ducts and glands in its frenzied rush to freedom. This chemical mélange is responsible for semen's peculiar yet elusive aroma, which can be affected by individual factors, such as diet. But the aromatic base notes are provided by our friends the amines, whose job, in this instance, is to protect the sperm by neutralizing the acidic environment of the vagina.

Ask people what semen smells like and you will get a variety of responses. But over time, certain words will appear again and again: *bleach*, *mild cheese*, *rancid butter*; less frequently people will describe semen as smelling *fishy* or *sweet*. Amines can produce any of those odors.

So, for our investigation, we can say: *Let X equal amine.* Time to turn our sights to Y.

How Très L.A.

After a decade of dispute, readers of Cecil Adams settled the sperm tree debate by popular acclaim, bestowing the laurels on the carob tree (*Ceratonia siliqua*). A common street tree throughout California, particularly in the south, this flowering, subtropical evergreen with long, oval leaves can grow over 30 feet tall and is, improbably enough, a relative of the garden pea. You can spot the family resemblance in the carob's large, slow-ripening seedpods that can be seen dangling off its branches at most times of the year.

The carob was much praised in the early days of food consciousness, when entrepreneurial hippies discovered that its dried and pounded seedpod could be made into a sweetish concoction that had somewhat fewer calories than chocolate, whose taste and texture it somewhat less resembled. Carob "chocolate" became a feature of '70s and '80s health food, right alongside rice cakes, bean sprouts, and whole-grain anything. In this pre-PowerBar era, carob also played the starring role, alongside nuts, grains, and dried fruit, in the high-energy staple known among backpackers as *gorp* and to everyone else as *trail mix*.

With its preference for sunshine and mild winters and its association with an obnoxious food fad, the carob is definitely an Angeleno at heart. But it was, of course, its smell that sealed the deal with voters. The mature seedpod of the carob is tough and tarry, and if you break it open it emits a sweet-earthy smell— much less pungent than blue cheese but more pronounced than Brie—with a soft bleach high note, which many find redolent of jizz. The male flowers produce an even stronger smell. The secret again lies in chemistry.

Butyric acid is a fatty acid that is present in certain plant oils and animal fats. It was first isolated in butter, which is how it derived its name (from the Greek *boutyros*). Butyric acid is found in nice things, like Parmesan cheese; useful things, like muscle plasma; and unpleasant things, like flatulence and body odor. It also constitutes about two percent of the seed pod of the carob tree.

A by-product of oxidation, butyric acid frequently lurks in things that are fermenting or decomposing—which also means that butyric acid is often seen in the company of amines. So we see that, even if the odoriferous chemicals in semen and the semen tree are not identical, their associations are very similar and their fragrance profiles broadly overlap—a sharply alkaline high note followed by a bass that is vaguely animal and fatty.

Whether that is a pleasant profile or not is a question best left to individual taste. We've already seen how amines are closely associated with rotting flesh and rancid fats. Nevertheless, many responders find the smell of semen to be agreeably antiseptic. On the other hand, many find both sperm and the sperm tree smell deeply unpleasant. On the other, other hand, from at least biblical times peoples of the Mediterranean have enjoyed eating carob seeds and have used them as a sweetener. Some biblical exegetes identify the *locust bean* mentioned in the Torah and the New Testament with the carob, which accounts for one of the tree's aliases, *St. John's Bread*. (There is also a tradition that maintains that the pods the Prodigal Son fed to his pigs during his gig as a swineherd were carobs.)

Butyric acid, in particular, is a chemical Jekyll and Hyde: With a little tweaking, it becomes *ethyl butyrate*, an ingredient in perfume and artificial fruit flavorings. But in its raw, concentrated form, butyric acid makes a powerful stink bomb, one that smells remarkably like vomit, causes instant nausea in any bystanders, and taints raw meat on contact.

In smell, as with so much else in life, there is a thin line between love and agony.

There is no shortage of carob trees in Los Angeles, but if you'd like to have a truly immersive experience, pay a visit to Elysian Park, near Dodger Stadium. On a warm October afternoon, when the Santa Ana winds are blowing and the carob blossoms are at their height, you can lounge at a picnic table in the Carob Tree Grove.

Be sure to bring a bag of trail mix.

Oregon

Poop: the Ultimate Human Artifact

WHAT: Prehistoric human coprolites

WHERE: University of Oregon, Eugene

Who were the first people to settle America, and when did they get here? These are questions that archeologists and anthropologists still have not resolved.

The oldest man-made objects ever found in the Americas are ancient stone tools that were unearthed in Clovis, New Mexico, in the 1930s. Scientists have dated them to about 13,000 years ago, or near the end of the last great ice age. But Clovis arrowheads are not the oldest traces of human beings on this continent.

In 2002, anthropologists exploring a system of caves near Paisley, Oregon, found an even older . . . um . . . human product. Among piles of bones from prehistoric camels, horses, and sheep, the explorers discovered six human *coprolites,* or fossilized poops. Carbon dating in the laboratory showed that the human droppings were 14,300 years old—more than a thousand years older than the stone tools from Clovis.

Your poop says a lot about you, like what you eat, whether you are male or female, how healthy you are, and where your ancestors came from. Evidence from the prehistoric poops taken from the Paisley caves tells us that the early Oregonians were well acquainted with the area they lived in. They ate local plants much like the vegetation that still grows in Oregon's hot central region, including desert parsley, a low-growing herb with an edible, carrot-like root. Animals on the menu included chipmunks and small birds like sage grouse. Scientists also found traces on the coprolites of a very fine thread, much like the kind we use to make our shirts today. This indicates that Ice Age settlers may have worn tailored, formfitting clothes—which conjures up a much more dapper picture than the skin-clad cavemen we often imagine hunting woolly mammoths on the frozen tundra and dragging their wives around by their hair.

Because poop is very fragile, coprolites are a rare and valuable find. Coprolites survive because they have lost all their water, a process that hardens them almost into stone. In fact the name *coprolite* comes from the Greek words meaning *poop* and *stone* (*kopros* + *lithos*). In order to study these desiccated poops, scientists must first return them to their soft and pliable original form. They do this by soaking the coprolites in a special solution. Once a coprolite is re-hydrated, scientists can poke around in it to find undigested objects, such as seeds and bones, and, if they are very lucky, they might even find DNA.

There is one downside to the soaking process, however: Wetting poop has the unfortunate side effect of reactivating its smell.

DNA analysis of the Paisley coprolites shows that the people who left them were related to ancient tribes that lived near Siberia. They probably looked a lot like Native Americans of today, but they were a little shorter—standing about five and a half feet tall. This gives support to the theory that the first American settlers walked here from Asia by crossing over a "land bridge" that connected northeastern Russia to Alaska and was exposed during the Ice Age when growing ice caps depleted water from the oceans.

With all the new facts coprolites have given us, it's no surprise that University of Oregon archeologist Dr. Dennis Jenkins has called these fossils "the ultimate artifact."

Fungus Humongous

WHAT: The world's largest fungus

WHERE: Strawberry Mountain, Oregon

Think fast: *What's the largest living thing on the planet?* (No fair looking right above; that's cheating.)

No, it's not the blue whale.

And it's not the mighty redwood tree, either. (But, good guess!)

In fact, the world's largest organism is neither animal nor plant, but a lowly parasitic fungus known to scientists as *Armillaria ostoyae*.

More commonly known as the *honey mushroom*, this fungus looks either like a very long, skinny button mushroom or a short, chubby, brown enoki. It likes to eat conifer trees, and is particularly dangerous to hemlock and Douglas fir, in which species it causes a disease known as *shoestring rot*.

A. ostoyae grows all over the western US, but the record-setting colony resides in Oregon, the soggy home to some of the nation's best mushroom land. This particular fungus is more than 2,400 years old and covers 3.5 square miles of forest. We can also call it 2,200 acres, which sounds even more impressive.

The disappointing part is that you can't see the fungus all at once. What we think of as a mushroom is actually just a fruit body, a small fraction of the fungus that pops up from beneath the earth or under tree bark to drop spores. Like an iceberg, however, most fungilogical action takes place under the surface. In *A. ostoyae*'s case, that means there are literally miles of stringy roots, called *rhizomorphs* (from the Greek *rhizoma* + *morphos*, or *root-shaped things*), that are continuously unspooling themselves underground. Having no chlorophyll, funguses cannot photosynthesize food from sunlight. Instead they must steal their nourishment from flesh and plants. *A. ostoyae* spreads its rhizomorphs surreptitiously through the soil of Strawberry Mountain, tapping one tree root after another in an ongoing act of subterranean piracy that has lasted for two and a half millennia.

Armillaria isn't deadly, but it can make you sick. While some fortunate individuals can eat it and experience no ill effects, it is best to leave it alone.

Washington

Look, but Don't Touch

WHAT: The Market Theater Gum Wall

WHERE: Pike Place Market, Seattle

The Market Theater Gum Wall

On Seattle's waterfront, beneath the Pike Place Market (home to the world-famous fish tossers and seat of the very first Starbucks), in a narrow walkway named *Post Alley*, you will find the city's celebrated *Gum Wall*, also known as the *Wall of Gum*.

Tradition dates its origin back to the early '90s, when list-less patrons queuing up for performances at an improv theater passed their time as they waited in line by sticking their chewing gum onto the alley wall. No, it doesn't make any sense. But there it is.

Old chewing gum and fresh fish don't mix, so the bosses at Pike Place Market eventually ordered the wall to be scraped clean. But the gum just came back again, and again. So, taking a cue from the local software industry, they turned a bug into a feature: By the advent of Y2K (that's cyberspeak for *the year 2000*) the Market Theater Gum Wall had become an official Seattle tourist attraction.

Now, it's a stupid gimmick to be sure, a wallful of other people's used chewing gum. Still, when you approach the multi-colored dots of fruit-flavored gum arrayed in broken patterns against the old brick warehouse walls, shimmering like a pointil-list painting, it is rather beautiful. You might almost imagine that you're looking at a shell-encrusted grotto in a Mannerist pleasure-palace dreamed up by some sixteenth-century Italian despot—if it weren't for the telltale chill rolling in from Puget Sound.

The wall can also just look like a spray of bird guano, if you're not in a poetic frame of mind.

The thickly packed expanse of gum that now stretches some 50 feet wide and 15 feet high was declared by CNN to be one of the world's germiest attractions. This inevitably lead to jealousy and backlash, as partisans of the suspiciously similar *Bubblegum Alley* in San Luis Obispo, California, defended their claim to that germy honor. The idea for Seattle's gum wall, like most of that city's population at this point, is, they argue, a California import.

Montana

A Rest(Room) for the Weary

WHAT: Lewis and Clark's latrines

WHERE: Travelers' Rest State Park, Lolo

This otherwise unremarkable grassy field on the banks of Lolo Creek has the singular distinction of being the only archeologically verified campsite of Lewis and Clark and their Corps of Discovery. Its number two distinction—if you will—is that the certainty of the verification rests primarily on the fact that Captain Lewis and crew pooped there. A lot.

On September 9, 1805, the thirty-three members of the Lewis and Clark expedition camped at a site they named *Travelers' Rest*. Although they did not realize it at the time, the explorers were about to begin the most difficult leg of their 4,000-mile journey from Illinois Territory to the Pacific coast—the portage through the Bitterroot Mountains, western Montana's stretch of the Rocky Mountain Range, where shallow waters would compel the men to carry their canoes for eleven days through dense forest and treacherous inclines slick from an early snowfall.

In his journal Meriwether Lewis described the campsite as

lying near the confluence of a small creek and the Bitterroot River. But in 2002, a close examination of historical documents combined with scientific soil analysis showed that the river had shifted over the centuries and that the site identified as Travelers' Rest by the National Parks Service in the 1950s was off by a mile.

The archeological evidence included traces of fire pits, a few trinkets, and, most decisive of all, latrines. A two-hundred-year-old latrine—which is essentially a pit dug in the forest floor—is not particularly easy to identify. But scientists had a definitive piece of evidence: elevated levels of mercury.

A deadly poison, mercury is not something typically found in human waste. So what was it doing there? And why did it indicate that these latrines were used by Lewis and Clark and not some other group of travelers?

Let us take a detour from the journey of Lewis and Clark now as we try to unravel the mystery of the mercury stool.

The Path from Pergamum . . .

Until the advent of televised political punditry, no one had a stronger claim to the title of World's Most Erring Professionals than did early physicians. With a limited understanding of the proper functioning of the body, the transmission of disease, or even the value of hygiene, doctors were unable to do much good for their patients and were capable of inflicting a good deal of unintended harm.

But to judge ancient doctors by our standards is perhaps unfair. In some ways, in fact, they were well out ahead of us, as, for instance, when it came to what we might call *wellness*—helping patients to maintain health and prevent illness from getting a foothold in the first place. Their universal prescription—eat little, drink less, get plenty of exercise and fresh air, and maintain a calm and optimistic outlook—is exactly the same advice you'd see in a glossy lifestyle magazine today and contains more wisdom than many diet books written today by people with MD after their name.

The controlling notion in antique medicine was moderation and balance, a concept we appreciate once again. But *balance* also had a technical meaning, which referred to a healthy internal interplay of what were conceived to be essential bodily fluids. That's where we part ways.

These essences were called *humors,* from the Greek *khymos,* meaning *juice.* There were four of them, and each had its distinct physical properties: *Blood* was warm and moist; *yellow bile,* also known as *choler* or *gall,* was warm and dry; *black bile* or *spleen* was cool and dry; and *phlegm,* aka snot, was cold and moist.

Each humor was also associated with a distinctive personality type. People characterized by blood were *sanguine,* generous and warm-hearted; *choleric* or *bilious* types had too much yellow bile, which made them quick to anger; excessive *melaina chole* (Greek for *black bile*) resulted in *melancholia* or depression; and *phlegmatic* individuals were stolid and dependable, if slightly cold and distant.

Slight variations in humors were the spice of life. But larger imbalances were believed to be the cause of sickness in all its diverse symptoms—chills or fever, sweats or constipation, bloat or sudden weight loss.

It is Hippocrates, a Greek physician who lived in the fifth century BCE, who receives the credit for first working out the details of medical humoralism, although the idea almost certainly went back at least several centuries before he wrote it down. But more than anyone else, it is a Roman physician named Galen of

Pergamum who was responsible for laying the four humors as the foundation of pre-modern medicine.

An excellent anatomist and surgeon in his own right, Galen fleshed out Hippocrates's writing with a wealth of firsthand, clinical observation. Galen was physician to three Roman emperors, starting with Marcus Aurelius, and when the great healer died, sometime around 201 CE, he left behind a vast body of medical writing that physicians for 1,500 years to come regarded as holy writ.

From Islamic Spain to Catholic Europe through to the Orthodox Eastern Roman Empire and all the way back to more Muslims in the Middle East, Galen was the unchallenged medical authority throughout the Middle Ages. His disciples, however, did allow themselves to "refine" the master's system, sometimes in ways that distorted the original almost beyond recognition and that often strayed far from the subject of bodies and medicine.

However elaborate the various teachings became, the essence of humor-based medicine always remained the same: maintaining an optimal balance among the four elemental fluids. Deficits could be overcome through eating foods thought to be rich in certain humors; and excesses were eliminated by purging. Today the archaic practice of bloodletting by means of leeches or surgical lancets is well remembered. But yesterday's doctors might also prescribe drugs that induced salivation or perspiration in order to purge the body of excess moisture; or emetics and enemas to discharge various biles.

... To the Portage Potties

As the scientific method took hold and a push for more empirical and rigorous medicine gained momentum in the seventeenth and eighteenth centuries, the weaknesses of humor theory became increasingly obvious.

Galen was on the way out, but, until **the germ theory of disease** gained acceptance in the late nineteenth century, there was no medical consensus to take its place. This intellectual vacuum led to a sort of Wild West moment, sometimes called the *age of heroic medicine*, when bold experimentation and aggressive treatment was the order of business.

The notion of bodily balance still endured, even though its theoretical underpinning had been rejected, and purging remained the favored treatment. But now doctors were swinging for the fences: not gentle aeration of the veins, but induced hemorrhaging until patients lost consciousness. A vogue for caustic heavy metals led to shudder-inducing treatments like mercury-vapor baths and **urethral irrigations** of silver nitrate. And purgatives were popped the way we take vitamins today.

It was at the tail end of this era of muscular medicine when President Jefferson was assembling the Corps of Discovery to investigate the continent that was opening up before the fledgling United States. Despite his well-known enthusiasm for science, Jefferson tended to regard physicians as airy theoreticians, untrained in the practicalities of field medicine and temperamentally unsuited to the hardships of the trail. Consequently he made no provision for attaching a medical officer to his expedition. He did, however, seek professional advice from Dr. Benjamin Rush, a fellow member of the American Philosophical Society (an organization over which Jefferson presided when he was not busy presiding over the nation) as well as a fellow Founding Father.

Like Thomas Jefferson, Benjamin Rush was one of those multifaceted Enlightenment thinkers who were seemingly everywhere at the time—the streets of Philadelphia alone were so full of them that you could hardly skip a stone without knocking the tricornered hats off the heads of two or three polymath geniuses. Rush was a medical doctor, a chemist, and a pioneer in the study and treatment of mental illness. He was friends with Tom Paine, enemies (for a time) with General Washington, and he signed the Declaration of Independence on behalf of Pennsylvania. Dr. Rush held what were then considered fringe ideas about the equality of the races, never shying away from speaking out as a full-throated abolitionist at a time when accommodation for the sake of national unity was regarded as the more statesman-like position on slavery.

Dr. Rush's social positions were progressive to the point of radicalism, but medically he was a Tory. He clung to the old-fashioned, Galenic concepts that were already passing away. And he was a great proponent of heroic doses of medicine, especially laxatives.

Dr. Rush obligingly drew up a few rules of health for the Corps of Discovery and provided Captain Lewis with a shopping list for what he considered the essentials of a first aid kit. On that list were at least nine different emetics, purgatives, and laxatives, including fifty dozen of Dr. Rush's own patented *Bilious Pills*.

About the size of a musket ball, the pills, popularly known as *thunderclappers*, were a compound of mercury chloride and jalap (*Ipomoea jalapa*), a variety of morning glory native to Mexico. On its own, each ingredient is a powerful laxative. In tandem, their effect is awe-inspiring.

Dr. Rush was convinced that what he understatedly called a "gentle opening of the bowels" would rid the body of toxins and thus prevent the onset of such maladies as colds, bronchial infection, smallpox, malaria, fever, body ache, and, oddly enough, dysentery. If one pill didn't suffice, you could take two or three.

Clearly, the corpsmen followed doctor's orders, because it is the mercury from Rush's thunderclappers that was discovered two hundred years later at the Travelers' Rest latrines.

As crazy as Dr. Rush's medical advice might seem today, it apparently served the expedition well enough. Only one man died during the two-year, 4,000-mile trek. It might even have accidentally been good medicine. Corps members went through periods of feast and famine, consuming up to eight pounds of meat a day, when game was available, and then foraging for berries and herbs where there was nothing else to eat. That's practically a recipe for constipation. Add to that the persistent problem of contaminated water, and it is no wonder that intestinal health was so well covered in the party's preparations.

See also:
Germ theory: Fecal transplantation therapy, Minnesota
Heroic medicine: The McDowell House, Kentucky
Urethral irrigation: Dough-Boy Prophylactic, Ohio

What's Your Poison?

WHAT: The Berkeley Pit

WHERE: Butte

Grossness is a matter of gut feeling, an irresistible surge of disgust that short-circuits thought and conscious judgment. It is a primal and primary experience—something we apprehend in that fraction of an instant even before the eye has quite grasped that it is looking at a maggoty dead eel or a soggy bag of poop or disembodied brains.

The Berkeley Pit

That's one of the most appealing aspects of the gross: its simple, irrefutable matter-of-factness. In a daily life fraught with second-guessing and choices with no clear answers, the sudden incursion of the gross is a refreshing instance when the body takes over and decides for us.

The Berkeley Pit is nothing like that.

An expanse of tranquil water four miles around and impossibly tinted a rich shade of cordovan red, the accidental man-made lake resembles an immense garnet recessed deep in a setting of dappled ochre rock. As luminous and vast as the lapis Montana sky above, it is a sight of unearthly, inhuman beauty.

It is only when you know that you are looking into an abandoned open-pit mine, the mammoth scar of what was once the nation's largest copper-extraction operation, and you begin to contemplate the degree of environmental damage that it takes to stain 40 billions gallons of water blood-red, that the feeling of queasiness sets in, a nausea that builds in proportion to the power of your imagination.

The Berkeley Pit is the thinking person's gross attraction. Possessing a grossness that resides chiefly in the mind of the beholder rather than the stomach, it is a sensation a philosopher might call *the sublimely gross.*

Nightmare Mixology

But gross it certainly is. The waters of the Berkeley Pit are so intensely polluted and so utterly still that they have settled into distinct layers, like a toxic pousse café—Campari red and Chartreuse green. The red is mostly rusty iron, which floats above a denser layer laden with copper. Arsenic, cadmium, zinc, and sulfuric acid lie throughout.

The brightly colored concoction of oxidized metals has the zesty acidity of a cola, and it packs a mighty wallop. Should you be so foolish as to drink it, the corrosive cocktail would blister your insides. Whatever hadn't leaked out of you as it corroded its way down through your throat and stomach would poison you many times over.

A misdirected flock of snow geese alighted on the shores of the pit back in 1995. The next day, 342 were dead. No fish swim here, no algae bloom. The stagnant waters are too toxic even to breed mosquitoes.

As lethal as it is lovely, the Berkeley Pit is the crown jewel of a 120-mile expanse of an ecological disaster area that stretches from Butte to Missoula. Rich in mineral wealth, including abundant veins of gold, silver, lead, coal, and above all copper, Montana enjoyed a mining boom that lasted from the end of the nineteenth century to the close of the twentieth. What remains today is the legacy of a land-use policy that was short on foresight and long on industry: The exhausted, contaminated, and discarded land now constitutes the nation's largest contiguous Superfund site.

Engineering Disaster

The word *mine* is likely to suggest images of shirtless men with blackened faces hacking out elaborate tunnel systems by the dim glow of lightbulbs stuck to their hard hats. But the Berkeley Pit, where ground was first broken in 1955, was a model of modernity that employed a relatively new technique called *strip mining*. This machine-intensive innovation uses massive explosions to blast down directly to the ore. Then mammoth earthmovers and dump trucks that can carry up to 200 tons of earth in a single load move in to haul away the ruined wrecks of toppled mountains and mining dross. Cheaper and easier than subterranean excavation, strip mining is also devastatingly effective.

In the twenty-seven years that the Berkeley Pit operated, more than 1 billion tons of earth were removed. An average of 17,000 tons of copper ore was mined every day. The operation was so intensive that, once it was brought to full speed in the early '60s, mining never once paused until the site was shut down for good in 1982. Ultimately the Berkeley Pit would swallow up a dozen older mines, as well as five outlying neighborhoods of Butte. Industrial mining was happening literally in people's backyards.

The pit was closed when it was no longer profitable. But it was not exhausted. When the pumps that kept the mine dry were turned off, ground water began to seep into the 1,800-foot-deep pit—or, rather, gush in at the rate of 6 million gallons a day. And it carried with it an alphabet soup of toxins, acids, and heavy metals leached out of the still ore-rich soil.

Today, the water level in the pit stands at just under 5,300 feet above sea level; at a point just above 5,400 feet, the flow will reverse and the toxic water will start draining out of the pit and into the groundwater that supplies Montana's largest city. A pump system is constantly monitored to prevent this from happening, while scientists and politicians try to find a practical way of cleaning up the mess.

Spare the Sludge

But now there may be an argument for *not* cleaning up the pit.

Contrary to any reasonable expectation, there are traces of life in the Berkeley Pit. And anything that can live there must have one hell of a story to tell.

In the mid-'90s, researchers from the University of Montana and Montana Tech discovered that a hardy alga called *Euglena mutabilis* was growing near the surface water of the pit. Its cheerful grass-green color belies the fact that *E. mutabilis* is perfectly content to bask in solutions of heavy metals that would kill other algae ten times over.

Creatures, like *E. mutabilis*, that can live in extreme environments—say in the boiling waters near deep-sea vents, or lightless, saline pools far underground, or in the hyper-polluted water of the Berkeley Pit—are called *extremophiles* (literally, *lovers of extremes*). The key to any extremophile's success is its adaptability. A rising toxic tide may have decimated the native microbial life in the Berkeley Pit—but it did not utterly eradicate it. A tiny number of genetic freaks were able to produce chemical compounds that protected them against the new, hostile environment, and, if they did not exactly flourish, at least they survived.

The thirty years of human time that have passed since mining ceased at the pit represents more than a thousand generations of algae and ten thousand generations of microbes. Over these generations, the survivors have adapted to become better and better at surviving. Meanwhile, other doughty colonizers have arrived, blown on the wind, drifting off bypassing birds, or trickling in with rainfall. All together, scientists have found 160 different species of extremophiles eking out an existence in the pit's toxic waters.

Some of these microorganisms do more than simply hold on and endure; they actually thrive in their toxic waste dump of a home. Algae such as *Chlorella ellipsoida vulgaris* consume heavy metals and, unwittingly, help purify the lake. Other unintentionally helpful species excrete bicarbonate waste, which, like a natural antacid tablet, reduces the acidity of the surrounding water. That, in turn, slows the chemical process that leaches more toxins into the pit.

One fungus unique to the Berkeley Pit has succeeded by learning to become meaner and more deadly than its competitors. This relative of the mold that gives us penicillin produces a chemical it uses to poison its foes. Dubbed *berkelic acid,* the secretion has also been shown to inhibit the growth of ovarian cancer. Another previously unknown mold has a slowing effect on lung cancer. Paradoxically, the deadly environment of one of the nation's worst toxic waste sites may hold a cure for one of nature's deadliest diseases.

Believe it or not, you can actually visit this gigantic Superfund site. To see how, go to the official Montana travel site (**visitmt .com**) and search for the Berkeley Pit.

Colorado

The Strange Saga of the "Frozen Dead Guy"

WHAT: Frozen Dead Guy Days

WHERE: Nederland

The Frozen Dead Guy Days parade

Perched in the foothills of Colorado's Rocky Mountains, the small town of Nederland can get up to ten months of snow a year. But for one resident, winter *never* ends. Grandpa Bredo Morstoel, aka *the Frozen Dead Guy*, is kept packed in dry ice in an outdoor shed, where he lies in a cryonic state, waiting to rise again.

At least that's the plan. But the people of Nederland aren't holding their breath.

Grandpa Bredo's story starts in Norway. Born near Oslo in 1900, Bredo lived a long, ordinary life until 1989, when he suffered a heart attack and died. That's when Bredo's story starts to get weird.

Bredo's body was claimed by his grandson, Trygve Bauge (pronounced *trig-VEH BOW-gay*), a Norwegian citizen who was living in Nederland, Colorado. Trygve had some very unusual beliefs. Among them was his conviction that cold temperatures can help you live longer. A great fan of ice-water swimming, Trygve founded the Boulder chapter of the Polar Bear Club, an international organization whose members go for a snowy outdoor swim every New Year's Day. Trygve claimed that in 1993 he set the world's record for the longest cold water swim. He reportedly stayed in for 65 minutes.

Trygve was also an avid enthusiast in *cryonics*. From the Greek word *kryos*, meaning *icy cold*, this controversial and highly experimental science seeks to extend human life span by holding people on the brink of death in a frozen state of suspended animation and then reviving them at some later date. It is based on the very simple and optimistic idea that medical science will eventually discover treatments for maladies that we cannot cure today. Here's how it works: Immediately after you die, you are submerged in a tank of liquid nitrogen. In a minus-320-degree-Fahrenheit nitrogen bath, you would be frozen so thoroughly that your body would never decay. One day in the future when a cure has been found for whatever ailment did you in, doctors could thaw you out, fix you up, and you could carry on with a brand-new lease on life. Voilà!

The catch—isn't there always a catch?—is that it's very tough to freeze a body without damaging it. Water expands when it turns to ice, as anyone knows who's left a can of soda in the freezer overnight only to come back and find an exploded mess. Scientists experimenting with cryonics have tried replacing the blood in their tissue samples with a sort of antifreeze that will remain liquid at very low temperatures. Naturally, that's not the kind of stuff you want pumping through your veins when you're awake and unfrozen, though. The alternative is simply to drain all your blood, which isn't a very happy solution either.

Even if we could freeze people perfectly, there's still the whole as-yet-unsolved problem of thawing them out and waking them up again. Clearly, the system has bugs.

But that hasn't stopped some three hundred people worldwide from paying somewhere in the neighborhood of $150,000, plus annual fees, to put themselves in frozen suspension at over a half a dozen cryonic centers. One of the more well-known sub-zero slumberers is baseball star Ted Williams, who has resided in Arizona's Alcor Life Extensions Foundation, the world's largest cryogenic facility, since his death in 2002. Alcor also houses the very first person to have been cryogenically frozen, James Bedford, a psychologist who was admitted in 1967 at age seventy-three.

Contrary to what you may have heard on the street, Walt Disney's body does not lie in cryogenic suspension, neither under the Pirates of the Caribbean ride nor anywhere else. His cremated remains are at Forest Lawn Cemetery in Glendale, California. (The inspiration for Evelyn Waugh's delightfully nasty Hollywood satire, *The Loved One,* Forest Lawn Cemetery is more vulgar than gross. But, while it may lie beyond the purview of this book, it is *definitely* worth a visit. If you're in Elysian Park paying homage to the sperm tree, do take the detour out to Glendale.)

Although a large proportion of cryogenic clients have been evicted from their nitrogen baths (typically because heirs tend to balk at the idea of paying indefinitely for the sustenance of loved ones who in every meaningful sense of the term have already died), no one has actually been revived from cryogenic suspension.

When Grandpa Bredo died, Trygve saw his opportunity to put his cryonic ideas into practice. The fact that he had no scientific training in no way daunted this inspired amateur. Grandpa Bredo was sent to a cryonic lab in California for temporary safekeeping, while Trygve set about building a cryonic facility of his own. After four years of labor, it was at last completed to Trygve's satisfaction, and Bredo moved into his new home in 1993. The accommodations were not as deluxe as what he'd been accustomed to in California. Instead of being kept in a tank of liquid nitrogen, he was put in a metal coffin in an ordinary tin toolshed and packed in dry ice. At minus 90 degrees, Bredo was uncomfortably warm for cryonic preservation, but he never complained.

The reunion between grandfather and grandson was unhappily brief. In 1994, Trygve was arrested by immigration officers. The visa that allowed him to stay in the US had expired, and technically he was a fugitive from justice.

It was during Trygve's immigration hearing that the people of Nederland found out about Grandpa Bredo. Trygve had never informed the local authorities about his makeshift cryonics lab, and it looked like the young man was about to get into some very deep trouble. But, contrary to everyone's expectation, there was no actual law in Nederland that forbade people from keeping their dead grandfathers frozen in a toolshed in their own back-yard. That legal oversight was soon corrected, but there was nothing the town council could do retroactively about Grandpa Bredo. The law compelled Trygve to go back to Norway, but Bredo was free to stay right where he was.

And there Grandpa Bredo stays. Trygve employs people to check up on Bredo regularly and repack him in dry ice. After a chilly reception that lingered for several years, the town eventually warmed up to their hundred-year-old orphan. The initial feelings of surprise and horror have been replaced with a playful affection for the Frozen Dead Guy.

Since 2002, the town has held a celebration in honor of Grandpa Bredo. Held in March, Frozen Dead Guy Days is like a late-winter Halloween. Children dress up like skeletons and adults race coffin sleds downhill or play games like bowling with frozen turkeys. The whimsically morbid festival, which makes light not only of death but of the long and harsh Rocky Mountain winter, is Nederland's way of celebrating life and welcoming the return of spring. Even Trygve approves. He has called Frozen Dead Guy Days "cryonics' first Mardi Gras."

Sound like fun? Then start planning your cryogenic pilgrimage at **frozendeadguydays.org**.

Because Tragedy Plus Time Equals Good Eats

WHAT: The Alferd Packer Memorial Restaurant and Grill

WHERE: University of Colorado, Boulder

Since 1968, CU–Boulder students have been paying homage to a notorious criminal with every visit to the student center. That's the year some member of the student council thought it would be a groovy idea to name the campus food court after Alferd Packer, Colorado's most infamous cannibal.

Capricious?—Yes. *Offensive?*—Meh. That's just what students were like in the 1960s. When they weren't protesting pointless wars or fighting racial intolerance, they enjoyed sticking it to the Man in more petty and ineffectual ways, such as by nominating Mickey Mouse for president or naming campus food courts after Old West anthropophagists.

Who was this Alferd Packer, the fellow with the dyslexic name and a taste for man flesh? There's not much to know.

In the winter of 1874, Packer enters history at the head of a six-man crew fated to become Colorado's own mini **Donner Party**. The men had been part of a larger company that left Utah in November intending to prospect for gold at the eastern foot of the Colorado Rockies. With snow falling and food in short supply, the main party sensibly chose to pass the winter at the *western* foot of the Rockies, in the care of a hospitable tribe of Indians. Packer and his breakaway band thought the others were just being crybabies about a little cold weather, and decided to rush the final leg of the journey. *More gold for us*, they thought.

What is one lesson you must absolutely take away from this

book? *Never* try to cross the snow-covered Rockies on foot under the mistaken notion that you'll be over before the bad weather *really* hits. You will die. Or you will be forced to eat the flesh of your dead companions, and then you'll probably die anyway. There is no other option.

It's like thinking that you'll just sneak your car under the railroad-crossing gate, because it would be a *total* drag to have to sit there while the freight train goes by. Sometimes it's better just to wait.

So, of course, Packer and his men got stuck in the snow and everyone but Packer died, and they got eaten, too. How exactly that happened, though, will never be known for sure, because there was only one witness—Packer himself—and he kept changing his story. Because, for some reason, people kept wanting to charge him with murder. In the final revision of his testimony, Packer put all the blame for the cannibalism on one deranged companion, whom he confessed to killing—but in self-defense, of course.

This explanation was found by a jury to be too self-serving to be credible, and Packer was convicted of murder. When the conviction was dismissed on appeal for lack of evidence, Packer was tried again. This time the charge stuck, and the man-eating manslaughterer was sentenced to forty years. After serving fourteen years, though, Packer was paroled on grounds of poor health. He died six years later, in 1907.

It is said that late in life, Alferd became a vegetarian. CU campus wags maintain that one visit to the Packer Grill might make you a vegetarian too.

See also:
Donner Party: Donner Memorial State Park, California

THE SOUTHWEST

Arizona

From Our Sewers to Their Slopes

WHAT: A mountain of reclaimed snow

WHERE: Arizona Snowbowl, Coconino National Forest

We all know better than to eat yellow snow—but is it OK to ski on it?

That's the question the National Forest Service, the Department of Agriculture, the Arizona Department of Environmental Quality, the city of Flagstaff, the Sierra Club, thirteen Hopi tribes, and one Arizona ski resort have been debating for more than five years.

Nestled in the San Francisco Peaks, the Arizona Snowbowl is one of the nation's oldest skiing attractions. It is also one of its driest. Ever since its first snowbirds made their debut runs in 1938, their winter-sporting pleasure has been held hostage by erratic snowfall.

Supplementing Mother Nature with a little human snowcraft would help stabilize the slopes and, by extension, the Flagstaff tourist industry. The problem, however, is that there is no reliable source of water in the San Francisco Peaks. Really. *None.* Not even underground.

However, the nearby city of Flagstaff is willing to deal. In the arid Southwest, drinking water is too valuable to spare, but the city does have some slightly used water that it's eager to move. The technical name for it is *reclaimed water,* and what it's been reclaimed from is the municipal sewer.

Water 101

Vapor gathers into clouds. The clouds condense into raindrops, which fall to earth to water thirsty animals and irrigate crops. The runoff drains into lakes and oceans, where the sun's heat warms the water molecules, and the liberated vapor rises up into the clouds to begin the process again.

That's the water cycle, and it has been nature's way ever since there was water to rain and living things to drink it. It might be gross to think that every sip of water we drink has been drunk and expelled countless times before, but there's really nothing to worry about: Nature does an excellent job of recycling. We can also take refuge in the fact that the environment is so vast an operation and with a production schedule so slow that we mere mortals can seldom catch a clear glimpse of what is really going on in the cosmic sausage factory.

Not so for the municipal sewer. It's very easy to see what goes on there and to contemplate the suggestive gap in the water cycle between use and reuse when we're talking about toilet to tap.

Briefly put, reclaimed water goes through three stages of purification. First, the dirty water is allowed to rest in large tanks so that heavy solids have time to settle and lighter oils to rise.

After these gross impurities are removed, the water moves on to step two . . .

Which starts with a vigorous churning, or *aeration*. The influx of oxygen stimulates microorganisms, which start breaking down suspended organic matter—yes, that means *sewage*, among other impurities such as food scraps and detergents. "Breaking down," in this context, means "eating it." And while the bacteria are doing their job of consumption, they expel methane and carbon dioxide gases, which escape by bubbling up through the water, and nitrogen-rich sludge, which settles to the bottom of the tank. In between is cleanish water.

After another settling, the treated water is filtered. Then chlorine is added to kill off those helpful microorganisms that have just broken down all that organic pollution but which, unfortunately, can also make us sick. (*Sorry, guys, but thanks for the hard work!*)

The treated water is now pretty good. Maybe even very good. But it's still not *drinkable* good.

It is in this last phase where the law of diminishing returns sets in. This well-known principle of economics dictates that, as any operation becomes more efficient, any further investment in improvement will net smaller and smaller margins of profit. In other words, at some point it is simply not worth the effort to make your product any better. And that is the doldrums in which water reclamation has been stuck for decades. Getting over the hump from *very good* to *kitchen grade* is not technically difficult—it's mostly just a matter of more filtering—but it is expensive and time consuming. While global trends indicate that drinking water may become a scarcer and more expensive commodity in the not-too-distant future, until its price actually does spike, most communities are unwilling to take that extra step and produce potable water.

So most recycled water stays in this *reclaimed* state.

Each state sets its own policy for how reclaimed water can be used. In Arizona, A+ grade reclaimed water is considered safe for irrigating crops and landscaping—like on golf courses and school athletic fields. It's OK for dairy animals to drink, but is not considered potable for people or pets. Reclaimed water is not considered fit for any home use whatsoever. It cannot be used in swimming pools, hot tubs, or showers, and it can't even be *indirectly* piped back into houses.

Now, Arizona law does not specifically mention the status of artificial snow—is it more like the field you play on, like a lawn, or a medium you are immersed in, like a swimming pool? This ambiguity has allowed parties who oppose the Snowbowl's modest proposal to make sewer-snow to appeal to the courts—which they did, once in 2005 and again in 2010.

Environmentalists argued that the risk of ingesting snow while skiing is high enough to disqualify reclaimed water from snowmaking. Attacking from a different angle, representatives of the Hopi nation have made the case that artificial snow of any kind would be a defilement of the San Francisco Peaks, which they consider sacred.

On both counts, Arizona judges sided with the sewer-snow. While the court acknowledged that Frankensnow might dampen "spiritual fulfillment," it would not place a "substantial burden" on the free exercise of religion in the San Francisco Peaks. Also, in the court's opinion, reclaimed snow clearly belongs under the rubric of *landscaping*, not *consumption*—though the judge added the wry proviso that falling skiers should try their best to avoid eating a mouthful of the stuff.

If these rulings are representative, Arizona judges sound kind of like snarky jerks. But they have a point. The controversy around the Snowbowl might be mostly a matter of perspective and comfort level. If, as some scientists and public policy experts believe, the planet is on the verge of a water crisis, then we all might have to do some recalibrating. Is it mere fastidiousness to worry about snow manufactured from treated sewage, when the slopes are already the outdoor potty for wild life and inconvenienced skiers?

Any reasonable calculus of risk must rate the possibility of breaking your neck in a downhill crash against the hazard of coming up again with a mouthful of pee-snow. If you're willing to accept the first, can the second be so horrible?

New Mexico

Sympathy for the Serpent

WHAT: American International Rattlesnake Museum

WHERE: Albuquerque

There is no denying that in the game of interspecies PR, snakes were dealt a losing hand. When members of the world's three major monotheistic religions blame you personally for banishing humankind from Paradise, you know you're in bad shape.

For countless other people though, the antipathy is visceral and not theological: Snakes just give them the heebie-jeebies.

The ambitiously, if oxymoronically, named American International Rattlesnake Museum is one man's attempt to even the scales, so to speak. Established by a former high school biology teacher, the museum presents exactly the blend of dorky earnestness and corny humor you would expect from a high school biology teacher. And that is precisely the right combination to help nervous herpetophobes slough off their anxiety and give these slippery sidewinders a second chance.

The museum boasts the largest collection of live rattlers in the world, outnumbering the displays at the Bronx, Philadelphia,

Denver, San Francisco, San Diego, and National zoos *combined.* Each species is displayed in a glass tank that simulates its natural environment, so the snakes feel right at home.

Not strictly limited to rattlesnakes, the museum throws in a few vipers, tarantulas, scorpions, and Gila monsters for good measure. The point is not to strive for purity, but to win some love for the whole maligned family of venomous animals.

Nevertheless, some of the exhibits, such as "Beverages with Animal Names on the Labels" (i.e., a shelf of microbrews with reptile-themed names), stretch the concept almost to the breaking point. But the cool quotient of oddities like the Edwardian opium casket carved in the shape of a skull with a viper crawling through the eye sockets cannot be denied.

The American International Rattlesnake Museum is open seven days a week. Check the website for current hours and admission prices: **www.rattlesnakes.com**.

Texas

Step Inside

WHAT: The Amazing Body Pavilion

WHERE: The Health Museum, Houston

Let's get this clear from the start—this is *nice* gross.

There are no scary old Victorian amputation saws, no diseased lungs in jars, no cross sections of human heads. This is a hands-on, interactive, primary-colored, *very* kid-friendly science museum that parents can feel safe bringing even a toddler to. But it's still about people's insides.

The highlight of the museum, as far as we are concerned, is the Amazing Body Pavilion, which takes families on a Texas-sized tour of a simulated human body. The main chamber is crowned by a 22-foot-long spine with ribs descending like pillars. Since it opened in 1996, more than one and a half million visitors have gaped at its 27-foot-long intestine, strolled through its supersized brain, and peeped through its colossal walk-in eyeball.

If you do crave something a touch *outré,* real-life cow eye dissections *are* on the menu, but you'll have to search them out amid cheerful displays and benign video kiosks that show simulated images of what you might look like older, or if you were a different sex.

Other distractions included brainteaser games, a sensory garden, as well as theater that shows 3D and 4D films (spoiler: the 4th D is *water*).

Think of this as your child's gateway drug to morbidity.

Find out more about the Health Museum at **www.mhms.org**.

"Every Day Above Ground Is a Good One"

WHAT: Civil War battlefield embalming diorama

WHERE: National Museum of Funeral History, Houston

Located in an ordinary-looking warehouse, this down-to-earth museum of funerary practices avoids the sensational and salacious aspects of its subject and instead looks at death with a professional eye. It houses an impressive display of unusual caskets (the long rectangles that appear at most modern funerals) and coffins (the more iconic, stretched-out hexagonal boxes). Highlights include a coffin made from glass and another commissioned to fit a family of four. There is also a display of fancifully decorated caskets from Ghana, claimed to be the largest outside of Africa, as well as exhibits on presidential and even papal funerals.

For most visitors, however, the scene-stealer is the museum's superlative exhibit of hearses, which comprises more than a dozen of both the horse-drawn and motor-driven varieties.

A less trafficked exhibit is a diorama that depicts a uniformed surgeon in a dilapidated Civil War tent. He is seated next to a recumbent figure shrouded in a white sheet out of which a rubber tube extends, terminating in a round pump the surgeon is squeezing in his right hand. The surgeon is laboring not to save the patient, but to preserve the corpse. The scene commemorates Dr. Thomas Holmes, the Father of Modern Embalming.

An Embalmer Is Born

A seminal figure in the world of undertaking, Dr. Holmes was a polarizing personality in his own time and is today a fascinating and undeservedly obscure character.

The details of Holmes's life story are fragmentary, and the facts, such as they are, are often skewed to suit either the prejudices of his detractors—of which he had many—or his own rather self-regarding point of view. However, the image that clearly emerges—one part grating self-promoter and two parts brilliant eccentric—is a portrait of a bona fide American genius.

Born in New York in 1817, Thomas Holmes enrolled in the College of Physicians and Surgeons, the city's first medical school (now part of Columbia University) at some point in the 1840s. Professors recalled him as a brilliant student, but it is unclear whether Holmes actually graduated. A story circulates that he was kicked out for the double-whammy of habitually experimenting on cadavers without authorization and then abandoning the bodies, scattering them absentmindedly throughout the institution. A more favorable spin maintains that the student was so focused on his research that he was apt to literally wander away with his thoughts, to the neglect of his cadavers, which were, after all, dead and beyond caring what happened to them. Whatever the explanation, this cavalier ease around the dead would be a trait that Holmes never outgrew.

With or without a medical degree, Holmes landed on his feet.

He found work as a medical examiner at the New York coroner's office and took to styling himself as Dr. Holmes. The city's booming murder rate in the mid-nineteenth century provided ample materials for the young doctor to continue the practical investigations whose overly zealous pursuit had preempted his formal education and would remain his lifelong obsession: the preservation of human bodies.

In Holmes's time, embalming was a niche interest confined mostly to anatomists, whose primary concern was maintaining the integrity of cadavers and specimens for medical research. Holmes mastered what literature there was on the subject of embalming, from classical sources that endorsed honey and beeswax to moderns who preferred the less wholesome path of arsenic and mercury. Working late nights at his home in Williamsburg, Brooklyn, he put his reading to the test on cadavers he brought back with him from his job at the coroner's office (which, mind-bogglingly, was perfectly legal back then). By 1850, Holmes had developed an effective embalming fluid that—despite being made largely from arsenic and zinc chloride—was significantly less toxic than anything else available at the time. No less important than his new recipe was his patented hand-pump delivery system, which allowed the fluid to be injected directly into the veins, greatly improving the ease and efficiency of embalming.

The Commoditization of Death

Death and decay were a source of endless fascination for Holmes. It is a matter of good luck, however, that he lived at the right moment to profit from his obsession.

Up until the mid-nineteenth century, rapid decomposition

had been part of the expected way of death. Since people tended to die at home near loved ones, an immediate funeral rarely presented a hardship. In cases when it did, undertakers could extend the time frame a bit by packing corpses in ice. But longer-term preservation—embalming—was regarded as, at best, an expensive novelty, an indulgence for princes and pontiffs, and, at worst, a pagan abomination, a holdover from the idolatrous ancient Egyptians, and a violation of the body, sacred vessel of the soul.

The Civil War changed all that. As young men conscripted to the cause began to die in unimaginable numbers on battlefields far from home, bereft families throughout the nation put aside their qualms and began to clamor for some way of reuniting with their fallen sons one last time.

Embalming suddenly had a market.

Scores of dodgy and slightly-less-dodgy "embalmer-surgeons" rushed into the void. Like vultures, they hovered around troops on the march, peppering them with flyers that described how their soon-to-be-dead bodies could be preserved for the comfort of loved ones back home, and at a reasonable price. Some entrepreneurs even embalmed unclaimed bodies and set them up near camps as advertisements.

Holmes never had to stoop to that level. Using his connections and a growing medical reputation, he successfully lobbied for the right to embalm the first high-profile casualty of the Civil War, Colonel Elmer Ellsworth. This former colleague and personal friend of President Lincoln was killed in defense of Alexandria, Virginia, at the head of the dashing all-firefighter militia that he had formed and personally trained: New York's flamboyant 11th Infantry, who adopted the baggy red genie pants of French North African legionnaires and were popularly known as

"Ellsworth's Fire Zouaves." The colonel died a hero and was to be honored by lying in state at the White House.

Holmes's celebrity embalming was an advertising coup of immeasurable value. And he made the most of it. Never shy about his talents, Holmes expounded at every opportunity on the excellences of his system and dismissed the ability of nearly every embalmer who wasn't himself. For the privilege of being treated by the self-styled Father of Modern Embalming, soldiers were charged double the going rate: Enlisted men paid $50 and officers $100—about $2,500 of purchasing power in today's dollars. Services included a coffin and transportation of the body.

Holmes would later reckon that he personally embalmed more than four thousand soldiers—including at least five generals—during the war.

After the armistice, Holmes returned to Brooklyn and ran a drugstore whose primary goods were a homemade root beer and his special embalming fluid, *Innominata* (Latin for *unnamed*), which sold for $3 a gallon. As an advertisement for the effectiveness of his Innominata, so it is reported, Holmes displayed in his shop the embalmed corpse of a fourteen-year-old girl that he claimed he had kept from decay for forty years.

But running the shop was almost an afterthought. Most of Holmes's energy was given to defending his title against the claims of usurping embalmers, and to refining his preservation techniques. To do that, he continued to study cadavers at home. When Holmes died in 1890, several embalmed corpses were discovered buried in his basement. Several more were actually found *inside* the house.

Ghoulish rumors circulated, but Holmes was posthumously cleared of any wrongdoing when proper documentation for the cadavers was provided. Evidently, the part about experimenting on them at home and then burying the arsenic-soaked human remains in the basement next to the casks of home-brewed root beer presented no criminal, health, or zoning problems in the libertarian paradise of the Gilded Age marketplace.

In accordance with his wishes, Holmes's body was not embalmed. This was not hypocrisy on his part or a sentimental longing for a natural death: Holmes had passionately maintained that he himself was the only competent embalmer in the nation, and he would have nothing but the best.

The National Museum of Funeral History is open seven days a week. Visit the website for hours and to keep up on the latest exhibits: **www.nmfh.org**.

See also:

Embalming/tissue preservation: Flameless cremation, Florida; Frozen Dead Guy Days, Colorado; Ward's Natural Science Establishment, New York

Corpses, acquisition and use of: Anthropodermic biblioplegy, Massachusetts; Cemetery gun, Pennsylvania

Where Every Roach Has Its Day

WHAT: Cockroach dioramas

WHERE: The Cockroach Hall of Fame and Museum, Plano

Michael Bohdan is the proprietor of the Pest Shop extermination service outside Dallas, Texas. He makes his living exterminating cockroaches, but that hasn't stopped him from developing a deep respect—even affection—for these tenacious and adaptive creatures that have been roaming the earth for more than 3 million years.

Thirty years ago, Bohdan held a contest to find the largest roach in Dallas. He took the more impressive entries (including the winner—which measures just under two inches!), mounted them in little display boxes, and hung them on the wall of his shop. Behold!—the Cockroach Hall of Fame and Museum was born.

The name may sound impressive, but the museum is just a section of Bohdan's pest control shop. And yet it's a gleaming beacon for the lowly and reviled roach.

In addition to the mounted specimens, Bohdan keeps a cage of very alive Madagascar hissing roaches. Whenever they feel threatened, these 3-inch-long armored beasts rear up aggressively and make a hissing noise by forcing air out of their sides. (It is believed that Madagascar hissers are the only insects to make noise exactly this way. Other bugs that make hissing sounds usually produce them by rubbing body parts together.)

But as alluring as these two exhibits may be, the real show-stealer of the museum is Bohdan's collection of cockroach dioramas. You can browse two dozen displays, including a roach windsurfing off a miniature Caribbean beach and a tiny Statue of Liberty proudly holding aloft a fat, brown bug in place of her usual torch. You might need to be over forty to recognize the celebrities behind such tributes as Marilyn Monroach, Ross Peroach, and Liberoachi. But the bizarre spectacle of a cockroach dressed in a flowing sequined cape and seated in front of a tiny piano is something that people of all ages can enjoy.

The Cockroach Hall of Fame is in The Pest Shop exterminators, 2231 W. 15th Street, Suite B, Plano, Texas. Call (972) 519-0355 for hours.

Oklahoma

An Empire of Roadkill

WHAT: Skull cleaning and articulation services

WHERE: Skulls Unlimited International, Oklahoma City

One of Skulls Unlimited's cryptozoology creations—an alien skull

If you want to be successful, listen to your heart. That's the motto of entrepreneur Jay Villemarette. And when his heart said *skulls,* Villemarette followed. From the time he collected his first skull—a dog's—at age seven, to the time at age fourteen when he boiled clean a bobcat skeleton in his kitchen while his mother was away, until today, when he moves two thousand skulls a month of every size and species, this is a man who took his passion and made it happen.

Now Villemarette heads a company that is the largest supplier of osteological specimens in the nation—possibly the world.

Since 1986, Skulls Unlimited has been selling bones from

practically anything that walks, swims, or flies. Under the company's fanciful cryptozoology offerings, you can get even "casts" from creatures most biologists believe never existed at all, like Bigfoot and the chupacabra.

But Villemarette is not just a distributor of osteological specimens—you could consider him a manufacturer as well. That is to say, if you don't see the bones you want among his wares, you can send in your own cadaver, in whatever condition, and he will make it into a shiny skeleton just for you.

He's Got a Bone to Pick

To make a good omelet requires breaking a lot of eggs. To make a skeleton, you have to render a lot of flesh. The work is hard, smelly, and definitely not for the squeamish. But skull cleaning is Villemarette's *specialité de maison.*

Most of the rending takes place in enormous cauldrons, where gallons of boiling water melt the flesh right off the bones. (The process is called **hydrolysis** and is a term you will become quite familiar with throughout these pages.) The Skulls Unlimited factory houses vats large enough to accommodate any creature up to a 4,000-pound whale. But before any skeletons-in-waiting take the plunge, they go through a preliminary processing step, which has the delightfully old-fashioned name *flensing.* This could be updated to the blandly technocratic phrase *mass tissue removal,* or we could just use the venerable and more familiar term *butchery.*

It seems impossibly low-tech, but the specimens are broken down mostly by hand. Once the Skulls Unlimited team has gotten in there and cut away all the skin, sinews, and easy-to-reach meat, it clears out any brains by means of a special brain-sucking vacuum, and, at last, the carcass is ready for its hydroly-sis bath.

In the course of a gentle boil, hydrogen molecules in the water work their magic, loosening the flesh and emulsifying the oils that would otherwise cling to the bones and turn them rancid.

Fished out and set on racks, the bones are left to cool and dry overnight. Then they are given over to tiny specialists who handle the delicate work removing the last, tenacious shreds of flesh: The bones are left inside glass fish tanks to spend a day or two in the company of *dermestid,* or *skin,* beetles. True surgeons of the insect world, ravenous dermestid larvae clean out every nook and crevice of the bones without marring their smooth sur-face. Less interested in gourmandizing than reproduction, adult dermestid beetles ignore the carcasses and devote themselves to keeping the colony up to size and ensuring that there is always a hungry brood awaiting the next arrival of bone.

A finishing soak in hydrogen peroxide sterilizes the bug-stripped skeletons and bleaches them a nice shade of ecru.

Now that every scrap of muscle, tendon, and cartilage is gone, the bones are pristine, but there is nothing to hold them together anymore. So the skeletons must be painstakingly re-articulated. That's the time-consuming part of the whole process. It also takes a lot of practice and expertise.

Human remains pose particular difficulties. There is, of course, a psychologically disturbing aspect to handling corpses. But, to speak with brutal objectivity, at a purely physical level, human bodies are simply grosser than those of other animals. We are extraordinarily greasy creatures—possibly because of our very strange diet, so heavy on fats, sugars, and salt—and that makes us extra messy and smelly to deal with. We even gross out the flesh-eating beetles, which prefer to dine on any carcasses other than ours.

Now if this operation seems a little ghoulish and ethically sketchy to you, be reassured that the bone trade is a regulated industry. Villemarette firmly maintains that all his specimens have been properly obtained. Aside from the hunting trophies submitted by customers, Villemarette works with no animals that were killed just for their coveted bones or pelts. In fact, his business is mostly based on scavenging. Many of his specimens are donations from zoos, ranches, or game preserves, gifts of animals that died of natural causes or from predation. He even processes roadkill.

Human remains have their own protocol—they cannot be sold to the general public, for example, and all scraps must be handled as medical waste. Much of the dignity of the process, however, rests on the preparer's own sense of decorum and professionalism. Our human laws actually have more to say about the way we treat other species than what we do to ourselves.

It's rather touching, if you look at it the right way.

In 2010, Villemarette opened an osteological museum next door to his processing plant. The collection of three hundred specimens bills itself as the largest private collection on public display, and, for the proud proprietor, it represents the culmination of a lifetime devoted to skeletal servicing. The Museum of Osteology is open seven days a week. For visitor information, go to **museumofosteology.org**.

See also:

Hydrolysis: Flameless cremation, Florida

THE MIDWEST

Missouri

Hair-Loom Pieces

WHAT: Hair mourning art

WHERE: Leila's Hair Museum, Independence

An example of hair jewelry

Hair—silky, wavy, bouncy, sexy, healthy *hair*—is a most coveted possession. So long as it is still attached to your head.

Once it falls off, it instantly becomes filth, food for the roaches and a squalid bed for the earwigs. Twisted in bristles, it makes brushes unshareable. Matted in shower drains, it is the fuel for innumerable instances of domestic discord.

If you want to hear some serious hair hate, talk to a stylist. They'll tell you how it gets in their eyes, up their nose, in their mouths, an unwelcome reminder of customers past. And few things are as exquisitely painful as a hair splinter.

One hairstylist, however, who is decidedly *not* a hair hater is Leila Cohoon (that's three syllables, *lee-EYE-luh,* not *LAY-luh*). For fifty years, Leila has collected antique hair artwork, an almost forgotten craft that was very popular throughout the nineteenth century. Today she owns more than two thousand examples of bracelets, necklaces, brooches, watch fobs, hat pins, and cuff links—some dating back as far back as the seventeenth century, and all made from human hair.

The ultra-fine strands of our hair make delicate and exquisitely intricate lace. Hair art is generally dark to black in color—however the hair may have appeared on the head—but it has an uncanny glow and sheen that is more than a little disconcerting. You can catch flashes of auburn, blue, and even green, and it is quite lovely once you get beyond the initial creep-out factor.

But the purpose of hair craft was only partially aesthetic. It was primarily intended to memorialize a loved one. Although wearing another person's hair may seem morbid, these intimate keepsakes were a tangible link to an absent loved one. In a time before photographs, they were a way of keeping memory alive. In some respects, they were even more powerful than pictures. After all, a photograph is only an image, but hair, at least to a degree, *is* that person.

Soldiers went to war with watch chains woven from their wife's hair, and sweethearts kept their soldier's lovelocks safe in brooches and cameos. But most hair art commemorated the dead. Aside from an opaque black stone called *jet*, hair bracelets, necklaces, and other adornments were considered the only jewelry appropriate to wear during mourning.

Most hair art is a form of *bobbin lace,* where weighted strands are woven around a woolen or wire base. The hair would have been harvested from receptacles kept at the dressing table, or it might have been shorn from a body after death. In either case, the lace could be made at home or shopped out to artisans.

The centerpieces of the Hair Museum are the mounted and framed hair wreaths that line the walls from floor to ceiling. Family history woven from hair, the horseshoe-shaped wreaths were made open-ended so that hair from successive generations could be added. Some are of astounding intricacy and beauty.

Hair is an excellent medium for a memorial. It is made of keratin, a tough, fibrous protein that is also found in fingernails, hooves, and snake scales. If it is kept dry, hair art will last indefinitely.

Thinking of weaving your way to Leila's? Then go to **leilashairmuseum.com** for all the details. If you can't make it to Missouri, you can view some spectacular pieces from Leila's collection at her online gallery.

See also:
Mourning art: Cemetery gun, Pennsylvania

The Mouse at War

WHAT: Mickey Mouse gas mask

WHERE: US Army Chemical Corps Museum, John B. Mahaffey Museum Complex, Fort Leonard Wood

You might have thought that chemical warfare was nothing more than a bad memory, kept alive only in the shell-shocked verse of the First World War poets who witnessed the slaughter at Ypres and the Somme. Although it does not loom as large as it once did, chemistry still does have a role in the modern military. In fact, it has its own unit, the Army Chemical Corps. And it has its own museum, too, a building that comprises six thousand items related to the history of chemical, biological, and radiological warfare.

"Does that include flame warfare?" you ask. Oh, yes it does!

A series of six rooms walks you through the history of the Chemical Corps, from the bare-knuckles, anything-goes days of World War I to the Incendiary Age of World War II and Korea, when poison gas was shoved aside by more flamboyant napalm and phosphorus shells, to Vietnam, which added to the arsenal the infamous defoliant and carcinogen known as *Agent Orange*.

Since legal and open poison gas warfare began and ended with the First World War, much of the subsequent work of the Chemical Corps has been precautionary, directed toward protecting troops and civilian populations against rogue states and terrorist cells that might be more inclined to flout the rules of war. So, much of the museum represents the—shall we say—more pacific work of the corps.

There are displays of radiation and biohazard suits. There is also a look back to the Cold War, the era of nuclear fallout shelters in shopping mall basements and of duck-and-cover drills, when grammar school students were taught that crouching under their desks and closing their eyes was a credible prophylactic against nuclear irradiation and/or incineration.

But the quintessential emblem of chemical warfare is and always will be the gas mask—the black rubber device with the round, plastic eyes and the long, respirator-tipped snout that makes the wearer look like a ghoulish Snoopy or one of the characters from *Mad* magazine's "Spy vs. Spy." In a large display case, you can trace the century-long development of this military item that, perhaps better than any other, embodies both the absurdity and terror of war.

But . . . what if there was a *special* gas mask—one designed, say, for children, one that could try to turn cowering in an air-raid shelter while waiting out a lung-searing poison gas attack directed at civilian population . . . into a fun game?!

Yeah, they've got that too.

It's a prototype of the *Mickey Mouse Gas Mask for children*— Disney-approved and manufactured by the Sun Rubber Company. And a rough prototype it is. Rushed into production just one month after the attack on Pearl Harbor, the mask's design is, frankly, pretty pathetic. It's just an orange mask with a stubby, mousy snout, held in place by black straps that pass over the head and around the neck. Limp round ears attached to the top straps are the strongest clue to the mask's identity. But confirmation comes from a yellow filtration canister that hangs from the chin and is emblazoned with *Mickey Mouse* in red letters beneath a three-quarter profile of the plucky cartoon critter.

To give the Sun Rubber Company its due, later models did a *much* better job capturing Mickey's image. Whether they worked to protect their young wearers from poisoning is another question: Fortunately, that feared urban gas attack on US soil never occurred.

Maybe *gross* isn't exactly the right word to describe a Disney-themed chemical warfare protection device. Maybe it's *disturbing.* Or maybe it's just really, really *sad.*

In any case, it's certainly eerie as hell—as are the rest of the bug-eyed yet expressionless visages of the various anti-chemical masks.

On the other hand, this is a display that rubber fetishists will absolutely *L-O-V-E*.

Find out more about the US Chemical Corps, now called the Chemical Corps Regimental Association, and its museum at **www.chemical-corps.org/cms/history/museum.html**.

Minnesota

Spamtown, USA

WHAT: The SPAM Museum

WHERE: Austin

> *Something Posing As Meat*
> *Shit, Pork, And haM*
> *Ham that failed the physical*

These are just an iceberg-tip of the unkind epigrams that have been aimed at SPAM. Since its debut in 1937, Hormel Food's most recognized product has been the butt of so many jokes that it is almost embarrassing to join in the chorus of hilarity. In a nation ridiculously polarized over so-called culture wars, SPAM seems to be the one thing every American has license to mock.

That's harsh treatment for a product that has provided cheap meat to under-resourced areas for more than seventy years—a product that fed the Allied forces during World War II, kept starvation at bay for thousands of refugees in Europe, Asia, and the Pacific Islands, and provided a respite from strict meat rationing here on the home front.

But if SPAM is universally derided, that's because it is also universally familiar. For many chopped-ham haters, the eye-rolling is tied to a bond forged at the childhood dinner table and charged with that powerful mix of affection and embarrassment that is usually reserved for family members.

It's that elusive campy line between love and shame that Hormel's SPAM Museum attempts—not altogether successfully—to walk. Enter through the wall of SPAM, which is just what it sounds like—a wall lined with 3,500 telltale blue-and-yellow cans; watch the short film *SPAM . . . A Love Story*; bulk up your recipe Rolodex at Chez SPAM; and check out SPAM history and trivia at the CyberDiner (you *know* it's techie because there's no space between the words).

Clearly the executives who oversee the museum have made the strategic decision to go along with the joke, but the brightly colored interior, the generic evocation of '50s kitsch, the belabored wackiness of the placards show that they are not quite sure what the joke *is*. What can you say in the face of such disarming cluelessness? To speak the truth would be monstrous.

And utterly useless.

"The Miracle Meat in a Can!"

SPAM was introduced to the world under the label *Hormel Spiced Ham*. But that lacked pep or zing or zip or whatever other ineffable X-factor products needed in the 1930s, so the makers held a renaming contest. New York stage actor Kenneth Daigneau won the $100 prize for his coinage, which might have been a *portmanteau* (or *squeezed-up combo*) of the words *spiced ham*. Or not. (The SPAM Museum circulates that story, but it does not vouch for its authenticity.) There is another fishy twist in this pork story: Daigneau was the brother of a Hormel vice president, so one might catch the faint aroma of nepotism in the publicity stunt.

The product rechristened SPAM is a blend of seasoned pork shoulder and ham. Sodium nitrite inhibits bacterial growth and keeps the meat from turning an unappetizing gray—instead, it remains an unnatural pink. Potato starch acts as a binder to keep the chopped meat from falling apart. When the starch cools after cooking, it thickens into a clear, gelatin-like substance.

Today, that sticky goo is an especially unappealing aspect of the SPAM mélange, but it didn't always register as gross. *Aspic*— clarified meat or fish stock thickened with gelatin—was considered highly sophisticated fare in the nineteenth century. The poshest tables on both sides of the Atlantic were proud to serve any number of chopped meats quiveringly suspended in a medium of chilled, gelatinous aspic.

Part of the dish's appeal was the rarity of gelatin, which could be obtained only by **hydrolysis**, or boiling down collagen-rich animal parts, like hooves, bone, and sinew, for hours. Dried gelatin could be purchased in sheets, but they were very difficult to work with.

In 1923, powdered gelatin branded as *Jell-O* hit grocery shelves, which put aspic within reach of any home cook. By the 1930s gelatin had become a nationwide food trend. So, far from being a strange sight, Hormel's accessible version of *aspic au jambon* would have been a welcome addition to the lean tables of Depression-era America.

Eventually, a profusion of Jell-O salads that were more inventive than delicious would debase the once noble aspic and push it down the path to oblivion since followed by other food fads like fondue and salad bars. (Though, who knows, perhaps the time is ripe for a resurrection? Keep an eye out for lunch trucks on the streets of Portland doling out servings of menudo in aspic, or trendy, Lower East Side aspic lounges . . .)

It was the Second World War that made SPAM into the branding behemoth it is today. Light, easy to ship and to store, and shelf-stable for years without refrigeration, SPAM was precisely the food product the War Department was looking for when the nation mobilized against the Axis powers in 1941. Where the American G.I. went, SPAM followed. From British airfields to the beaches of Normandy to tropical islands in the Pacific Theater, some 150 million pounds of SPAM worked its way across the globe.

SPAM's postwar legacy still lingers. In Britain, where food rationing continued until 1954, SPAM became a staple. In fact, it became such a part of British life that the iconic piece of SPAM mockery comes not from the US but the UK: Monty Python's 1970 television sketch involving a fussy customer, a Viking chorus, and a diner that serves practically nothing but SPAM.

Today Guam is the world's largest SPAM consumer, with every inhabitant eating on average sixteen cans per year. Second place goes to Hawai'i, where restaurants proudly serve the local specialties, SPAM sushi and SPAM-garnished ramen.

In light of all the criticism, it's hard not to feel a twinge of sympathy for Hormel's most infamous product.

Still, the stuff *is* gross.

Find out more about the SPAM Museum at **www.spam.com/spam-101/the-spam-museum**.

See also:
Hydrolysis: Flameless cremation, Florida

A Stink by Any Other Name

WHAT: Corpse flower

WHERE: Linnaeus Arboretum, Gustavus Augustus College, St. Peter

> *Dead mouse*
> *Dead rotting meat*
> *Worse than a pig barn*
> *A college dorm room in May*
> *Bl-ee-a-ch-h-h-h! But beautiful!*

No, that is not a scatological haiku, but a sample of prose responses that visitors to the Linnaeus Arboretum left in the guestbook after meeting Perry. *Perry* is the arboretum's nickname for a very special plant, a rare specimen of *Amorphophallus titanum,* or *Sumatran corpse flower.*

The corpse flower, beginning to bloom

The expressive name is not the only striking feature of this all-around remarkable species. Consisting of a single, enormous stalk crowned by a single, enormous crinkly leaf, the corpse flower easily tops six feet in height and produces the world's largest blossoms. It is also a most temperamental and unpredictable plant that can take up to fifteen years to produce its first bloom. In the past century hothouses across the globe have managed to coax only about one hundred blossoms from this intractable plant species.

But the preeminent source of the corpse flower's fame is it unspeakable stench, which uncannily resembles the aroma of decaying flesh.

The corpse flower grows naturally only in the tropical rainforests of Indonesia, where it was first scientifically documented by the Italian botanist Odoardo Beccari in 1887. The locals called this noisome plant the *corpse flower—bunga bangkai*, in their language—but the foreign explorer dubbed it *Amorphophallus titanum*—or *gigantic misshapen penis*—because of its blossom, whose central spike upwardly thrusting from a frilly-edged sheath looks sort of like a gigantic, misshapen penis—if you have a dirty mind, which evidently Signor Beccari did.

The Victorian British, who grew the world's first cultivated corpse flower in 1889, apparently saw the similarity as well, because officials at London's Kew Gardens barred ladies from viewing the corpse flower's provocative blossom. But, of course, the Victorians are infamous for their filthy minds.

Ever since humankind has had tongue to speak, poets have compared their loves to fragrant violets and red, red roses. So it strikes us as something deeply unnatural for a flower not merely to smell bad, but to head-spinningly, eye-wateringly, teeth-clenchingly, gut-wrenchingly, lunch-hurlingly *reek. What, we gasp, can possibly be the meaning of* that? As is invariably the case with such questions, the answer is: reproduction.

You might catch more flies with honey than with vinegar, as

the saying goes, but an entomologist will tell you that you attract more beetles with rotten flesh than with rose petals. And it is precisely such carrion-eating insects that the corpse flower must attract if it wants to spread its pollen to other eligible corpse flowers.

Although the word *flower* is right there in its name, the blossom of the corpse flower is technically not a flower at all, but something botanists call an *inflorescence*, which is a collection of small flowers that look like one great big one. A more familiar example of an inflorescence is an ear of corn, which starts out as a cluster of many tiny flowers, each of which develops into an individual kernel.

Like the cob of an ear of corn, the corpse flower's central spike, or *spadix,* is a kind of shoot that produces hundreds of tiny flowers around its base. While corn takes care of its reproduction by catching pollen blown about by the wind, the corpse flower relies on the intercession of insects. Its appalling stink lures beetles and flies seeking a feast of rotting flesh deep into its inflorescence, where they inadvertently pick up pollen by tracking though the clustering flowers. When the disappointed scavenger insects move on to the next plant, they bring a fertilizing trail of pollen with them.

Each winter, the corpse flower dies down to a tuber, like a tulip or a crocus. In the spring, the plant sends up a stalk enfolded in an enormous frilly leaf. Then, if conditions are just right, every few years or so a spadix will shoot out of the plant's stem, which indicates the corpse plant is about to bloom. Since this is a rare event, botanists monitor their corpse flowers very closely in the spring and summer.

The Linnaeus Arboretum has set up a blog (**arboretum.blog .gustavus.edu**) that lets you know when their corpse flower is getting ready to bloom. If you can't get out to see Perry in person, you can at least watch online from home on their webcam (**gus tavus.edu/biology/titanarum**). But until someone invents smell-o-vision, home viewers will be missing half the experience.

The Crappiest Medicine Ever

WHAT: Fecal transplantation therapy

WHERE: Digestive Health Center, Duluth Clinic, Duluth

Pop quiz! We've come far enough along in our journey into grossness that now might be an opportune moment to assess our knowledge of all things taboo.

What are the top *don'ts* that everyone must respect in order to remain in good standing as a member of society? Go ahead and shout them out. Don't be shy!

—*Don't eat human flesh.* Yes, good one!

—*Don't keep dead people in your home.* Check!

—*Don't sleep with a close family member.* Yuck, yuck! Definitely!

—*Don't eat poo.* Well, you might want to reconsider that one. . . . An emerging therapy is challenging that last bit of common sense. It's called *fecal transplantation*, and, following the theory that one nail drives another one out, it aims to tame the unruly microorganisms in our guts by supplementing them with *more* microorganisms, from poo.

First tried in the 1950s, fecal transplantation, which consists of piping liquefied feces directly into a patient's intestines, debuted to shockingly little fanfare. But within the last ten years this rising therapy has really started to demand attention, moving quickly from a sick joke to a viable therapy.

Although there is still not a great body of research backing it up, fecal transplantation has scored enough successes that it can no longer simply be pooh-poohed.

A Desperate Measure for Desperate Times

What is it that could induce someone to try such an unsavory intervention? The answer: *Clostridium difficile.*

C. difficile—*C. diff* to those in the medical biz—is one of the many bacteria that live in our guts. Under normal conditions you would never know it is there. But in certain circumstances, *C. diff* starts to run utterly amok and causes all sorts of havoc, like aches, fever, debilitating diarrhea, blood poisoning, and even kidney failure. Each year, this microscopic frenemy of the human body makes about half a million Americans sick and is responsible for up to 20,000 deaths.

Cases of *C. diff* are especially common in post-surgery patients. The reason for this is the antibiotics administered to bolster the weakened immune systems of these convalescents. The most powerful antibiotics indiscriminately kill more or less every microorganism they come across, the good ones along with the harmful ones, which decimates the flora inside our bodies. But *C. diff* has developed resistance in the form of particularly hardy spores that spring back to life quickly after the antibiotics have run their course. They also proliferate quickly and at the expense of all the other microbes a healthy gut needs. Sensing, quite correctly, that it has been under assault, resurgent *C. diff* defensively lashes out extra hard against everything it comes up against, and this, it is thought, causes the unpleasant and dangerous symptoms associated with an outbreak of *C. diff.*

Repeated courses of antibiotics can give sufferers a respite, but, paradoxically, this just reduces the number of good bacteria and keeps the conditions right for a whole new outbreak of C. diff.

The idea behind fecal transplantation—also known as *biotherapy*—is to break this cycle of C. *diff* dominance by repopulating the gut all at once with its natural flora and, thus, restoring its microbial equilibrium.

This approach to bacteria is a major departure from what has been standard medical practice for more than a century. Since Louis Pasteur demonstrated back in 1862 that boiling milk could prevent salmonella contamination, the story of bacteria has been a simple one: Find bacteria, kill them, end of story. That's the *germ theory of disease* in a nutshell. And it has made possible so many of the advances that make modern medicine so much safer and more effective than ever before—innovations like disinfectants and antibiotics that make advanced surgery possible.

But this story is being rewritten, heralding perhaps a revolution in the way scientists conceive of the human body. Post-Pasteur, doctors pictured the body as an organic whole, self-contained and locked in perpetual struggle against invading hordes of bacteria and viruses. Recent discoveries in microbiology, however, seem to indicate that the body is more like an ecosystem. Each of us is like our own planet earth. The varied microclimates of our bodily geography host a vast array of microscopic life forms in a community known in its entirety as a *microbiome*. Some of our guests are indeed harmful, but many are vital to our survival. They support us, and we in turn provide them food and a home.

The World Inside You

As many as ninety percent of the cells in your body are not yours at all. They are bacteria, primitive single-celled creatures that abound in a staggering profusion. In your gut, for example, your most coveted piece of real estate, there are—right at this instant—somewhere around 100 trillion bacteria, representing perhaps 40,000 distinct species. There are so many of them that scientists haven't even named them all, let alone figured out what they do.

We acquire these microscopic menageries, our individual microbiomes, all on our own over the course of our lives. As babies we are born sterile, but are quickly colonized by microbial life. Even the way we exit our mothers affects this process—infants removed through caesarean incisions pick up different sets of bacteria than do babies who leave their mothers the old-fashioned way. The particular blend of organic life each of us supports is as unique as our thumbprint.

No matter how often you wash up or douse yourself in hand sanitizer, there is no place on you or in you that will remain sterile for long. Your nose, your mouth, your eyebrows, the crook of your arms, the back of your knees, your lungs, your belly button are all teeming with microbial life so diverse and so adapted to their particular locale that you might find them just there and no other place. One bacterium might like your right hand, but never look twice at your left; another might stake a claim to your molar but shun your bicuspid.

They are not just freeloaders, either. Bacteria do a lot of our digestion for us, for example. In fact, we'd starve without them. They take things that are difficult to digest, like starchy plants with tough cell walls, and break them down for us, exacting a caloric surcharge for their service. Regardless of what we eat for dinner, much of what our bodies *actually* digest has first passed through the flora that reside in our guts. In other words: It's bacteria poop.

Microbes are also essential in the development and healthy functioning of our immune system. But the details are still far from being understood.

A Prescription for Poop

As of yet there is no orthodox way of implementing the highly unorthodox procedure of fecal transplantation. Duluth's Digestive Health Center is one of the few hospitals that routinely practice biotherapy. In the past decade, they've done at least sixty-four fecal transplants, and the procedure they use is relatively simple. Once a donation is dumped off (usually provided by a spouse or close relative, someone who would likely have a similar blend of microorganisms as the patient's), the staff give it a light cleaning to filter out all the undigested bits of food. What remains is a watery mystery mix, each gram of which can contain tens of thousands of bacteria and millions of viruses. The cure is administered by pumping a few teaspoons through a tube into the patient's stomach, either down through the nose or up from the other end.

A higher-tech alternative is to spin the filtered feces in a centrifuge, until all that's left is a solid pellet. But effective biotherapy doesn't need a lot of bells and whistles. In fact, it can be simple enough to try at home—although I won't tell you how, because I don't want to be even remotely responsible for any ambitious weekend warriors out there who might decide to try their hand at DIY gastroenterology. If you must play with poo, stick to the kind that comes from cattle and go fertilize your vegetable garden.

Take Two Laxatives and Call Me in the Morning

So what are the exact biochemical steps that turn *C. difficile* from peaceable citizen of our internal community into an intestinal vandal? What is it that makes bacteria snap?

The full answer is still to be discovered—what we don't know about bacteria dwarfs the few things we do. But simply framing the question this way marks what could be a major shift in medical perspective away from concepts like *eradication* and *sterilization* and toward *management, ecology,* and *balance.*

But wait a minute—*balance? intestinal health?* Haven't we heard this all somewhere before? In the endless pendulum swing that marks intellectual progress, this seems an uncanny yet almost predictable return to elements of long-discredited **Galenic medicine**, when the concept of good health depended on the maintaining of a harmony among bodily "essences" and when purging was the most common prescription.

Fecal transplantation is hard enough to get used to. Let's hope physicians don't start to take a second look at **bloodletting** and therapeutic **enemas**.

See also:
Galenic medicine, enemas, bloodletting: Lewis and Clark's latrines, Montana

Illinois

STD Rex?

WHAT: The corroded mandible of Sue the Tyrannosaur

WHERE: The Field Museum, Chicago

Chicago's **Field Museum** is one of the nation's oldest and largest natural history museums. And since the year 2000, this venerable institution has been the home of one of the world's oldest, largest, and most beloved fossils, specimen FMNH PR 2081, better known as Sue the *Tyrannosaurus rex*.

Sue is named after paleontologist Sue Hendrickson, who unearthed the prodigious fossil at a dig in western South Dakota in 1990. Although the remains showed evidence of a hard life—including fractured ribs, an arthritic tail, and a heavily corroded jaw—the 67-million-year-old skeleton was more than 90 percent intact, making Sue the most complete *T. rex* ever found. Measuring 42 feet from snout to tail tip and standing 12 feet tall, she was also—and remains—one of the largest.

Sue was acquired at auction by the Field Museum, which paid a record-breaking $8.36 million for her—yet another first in the list of superlatives in Sue's résumé. In the decade since she was unveiled to the public, Sue has received more than 16 million visitors and is probably the only fossil known by name to every seven-year-old in the nation. However, medical researchers have unearthed a skeleton in her closet: Did skanky Sue die from an STD?

A team of scientists headed by a veterinarian from the University of Wisconsin, Madison, has studied the deformed jaw bones (or *mandibles*, as they insist on calling them) of a number of *T. rex*es, including Sue. They argue that the bone lesions are the work of a parasite, the prehistoric ancestor of *Trichomonas gallinae*, a protozoan which today afflicts certain species of birds, including raptors, like hawks and falcons, as well as more familiar, culinary breeds, like turkeys, chickens, and squabs. The single-celled invaders produce "cheesy," pus-exuding cankers in the mouth and throat of their unhappy hosts that eventually kill them. *T. gallinae* (which means something like *hairy single-celled creature of the chicken-favoring kind*) is closely related to the sexually transmitted human disease *Trichomonas vaginalis* (which means exactly what it looks like), an irritating but, fortunately for us, not especially dangerous infection of the reproductive system.

Your Lair or Mine, Baby?

It is altogether too easy to think that STDs are somehow fundamentally different from other diseases—not so much the result of bad luck as a shameful, personal indictment of our bad behavior. And since people are the only creatures who can be willfully bad, the idea of animal STDs can seem almost absurd.

That is an example of the *anthropomorphic fallacy*, an error in thinking that assigns human motives to nonhuman agents, like germs. It helps to recall that the diseases themselves don't care how they are transmitted; they simply find weakness and exploit it—whether it is an invitingly open wound or the moist and hospitable mucous membranes of the nose, eyes, or urethra, germs don't care: They just see a nice home.

Actually, they *don't* see a nice home. That is another example of anthropomorphic thinking. Germs just get busy eating and reproducing and don't think about it at all. Because that's what they do.

Human beings are by no means unique in being plagued by venereal disease. Mammals, insects, reptiles, birds, fish— anything that reproduces sexually can fall prey to STDs. Even flowering plants are susceptible to a variety of fungal *smuts* or *rusts* that shrivel their blossoms and rot their grains.

The most common STD in animals today is *brucellosis*, or *undulant fever*. It attacks cattle, camels, goats, pigs, dogs, deer, rats, and other mammals. Its most common symptom is miscarriage, but in some hosts it causes genital swelling and eye infections. People can catch brucellosis by drinking the milk or eating the meat of infected animals (or by having sex with them). In us, the disease causes flu-like symptoms that, without treatment, can last for years.

Chlamydia is an STD that attacks both people and animals, although we are each susceptible to different strains. As much as half of Australia's koala population is suffering from marsupial clap.

The human STDs gonorrhea and syphilis both came to us from cattle or sheep, possibly through sexual contact. In fact, many human diseases have migrated to us from our livestock—and from purely casual contact, nothing necessarily steamy or illicit.

The close relationship between Old World peoples and their livestock has historically been a natural laboratory for developing new diseases, but, on the upside, it has also fostered a robust immune system. The livestock-raising Europeans who colonized the New World brought their many cross-species germs with them, while the indigenous people of North America, whose only domesticated animals were dogs and turkeys, had no natural resistance to these foreign invaders. This is why it was the Native Americans who died from European diseases and not the other way around.

Prehistoric Sue might have caught a dose of primeval clap from intimate contact with another *T. rex,* but she could just as easily have contracted the disease from eating infected prey or even drinking polluted water. Her infection was so advanced that scientists believe Sue would have been unable to eat. In a sad irony, the mightiest carnivore ever discovered probably starved to death.

For more information, visit **fieldmuseum.org**.

See also:
The Field Museum: Ward's Natural Science Establishment, New York

Top Town for Faux Barf

WHAT: "Whoops" brand fake vomit

WHERE: FUN Inc., Chicago

It is instantly recognizable: a 5-inch disc of latex and foam, whose glistening, irregular features mimic the lumpy contours of half-digested food awash in a pool of a mysterious, ochre-colored liquid. But less well known is its name. Whoops brand fake vomit is an icon in the world of novelty gags—right there beside the Whoopie cushion, X-Ray Specs, and soap that turns your hands black.

A singularly scatological prank in the more staid days of joy buzzers and water-squirting boutonnieres, Whoops earned its niche in history by being one of the first novelties to cross the line from questionable taste to downright disgusting. It's a true American classic.

The world's most famous artificial barf was dreamed up about fifty years ago by an anonymous employee of Chicago-based toy designer Marvin Glass. Glass—the man behind such beloved and family-friendly games as Mouse Trap, Mystery Date, and Rock 'Em Sock 'Em Robots—was appalled by the concept. Fortunately for history, the people at rival novelty supplier H. Fishlove & Co. were possessed of greater intestinal fortitude. Proclaiming it genius, they licensed the artificial throw-up, and soon Whoops joined H. Fishlove's roster, right beside the windup chattering teeth known as *Yakity-Yak* and outlandishly outsized sunglasses called *Spectaculars*. Whoops's bold red package said it all: "The most disgusting laff getter!"

In the early 1960s—the heyday of fake vomit—some 60,000

Whoopses were manufactured every year. Today that number has dwindled down to about a tenth. Although there are rivals in the artificial barf market, Whoops remains the sentimental favorite, and experts in the field praise its quality and design.

In 1992, H. Fishlove & Co. was bought by FUN Inc., a marketing juggernaut that is the nation's largest manufacturer and distributor of novelties and magic tricks. But Whoops is still manufactured in the old Fishlove plant. Each batch of the latex concoction is mixed according to a secret recipe. It is lovingly ladled out by hand, dried, and packaged—all in a single brick warehouse in Chicago, which can rightfully claim the title of the world's capital of fake vomit.

Indiana

It's All in Your Head

WHAT: Syphilitic brains

WHERE: Indiana Museum of Medical History, Indianapolis

Built in 1896, the site that houses Indianapolis's medical museum is known as the *Old Pathology Building*—which might be an understatement, for this red-brick monument to late-Victorian science is Indiana's first pathological laboratory and one of the oldest in the entire nation. While the Indiana Museum of Medical History has all the usual antique medical equipment, outdated textbooks, and obsolete learning tools you would expect in any tribute to late nineteenth-century doctoring, what makes it something spectacular is the museum building itself, which has been meticulously restored and outfitted as it was in its glory days.

The Gross World of Gross Pathology

Starting from about the mid-eighteenth century, *pathology*, or the study and diagnosis of disease, was conducted mostly through

gross dissection of human cadavers. The word *gross* in this instance does not reflect a value judgment, as it does elsewhere in this book, but is used in its other sense, *large-scale*. In Enlightenment-era medical schools, students learned about the human body and its diseases by cutting up whole cadavers or by watching master surgeons perform autopsies in medical amphitheaters that could accommodate entire classes.

Early American research institutions, like the **Philadelphia College of Physicians** and the **Army Field Museum**, preserved examples of healthy and diseased organs and even whole bodies, which they stored in archives called *pathological cabinets* that could be consulted like a life-sized medical reference book.

But medicine changes almost like fashion, and by the late nineteenth century, *micro* had become new *gross*. In the wake of Louis Pasteur's groundbreaking work in **germ theory**, ambitious physicians began to turn away from large-scale dissection and started peering into microscopes and clocking hours in the chemistry lab.

In the new fields of *bacteriology* and *histology*, clinical researchers began to seek the origins of disease in microorganisms and in the microscopic anatomy of animal cells. Instead of examining whole bodies or organs, physicians scrutinized tiny samples under microscopes to look for irregularities at the cellular level.

Eager to attract gifted students and prestigious endowments, hospitals raced to build the most modern and high-tech facilities that would house a comprehensive range of cutting-edge pathological research. Indiana's Old Pathology Building was one of the first to achieve that aim. It had it all, from bacteriology, histology, and photography laboratories to an operating theater and autopsy room to a chemical storage room to library and records rooms to even a funeral parlor and morgue. (These last rooms were necessary because they were an instrumental part of obtaining specimens: The families of deceased patients were offered free funerals for their loved ones, if they consented to donate the bodies to science first.)

Gross dissection might have been losing relevance in 1896, but today the dissection theater of the Old Pathology Building, with its soaring ceilings, white plaster walls, and honey-wood moldings, is still mighty impressive. Semicircular tiers arrayed with Shaker-style cane chairs rise up two stories to look down on a blackboard and speaker's lectern, while, from above, large skylights bathe the interior in sunshine. It is a bright, neat, and streamlined space that is the antithesis of the lush and clubby interiors of earlier medical Victoriana. (See the **New Orleans Pharmacy Museum** for an example of the latter.)

Before 1932, when the operating theater was converted into a lecture hall, the lectern would have been replaced by a large bed of perforated steel called an *autopsy table*. The table was perforated so that the fluids from the dissected bodies would flow straight down and not drip over the edges of the table and onto the surgeon's shoes. Today, the white tiled floor and the incongruous drain near the blackboard are the only traces of this ghoulish past.

Illness of the Mind

The Old Pathology Building was commissioned as the research wing of the now defunct Central State Hospital, Indiana's first psychiatric institution—or *lunatic asylum*, as they preferred to call them at the time.

Central State Hospital started out in 1848 as the Indiana State

Hospital for the Insane. The *insane* eventually dropped out of its name, but never its function. For a century and a half, until the hospital's closing in 1994, the institution's primary focus was *psychopathology,* the physiological treatment of psychological disorders. In their new, state-of-the-art laboratory, doctors at the hospital hoped to discover the physical roots of mental illness, in either natural deformities of the brain or injuries to it from trauma or disease.

If you consult one of the old patient rosters, you will see that inmates suffered from a wide variety of maladies we still recognize today—anxiety, depression, post-traumatic stress disorder (known then as *Mexican War excitement*), epilepsy, alcoholism— as well as many we don't, such as religious excitement, excessive lactation, adultery, dissipation, masturbation, gourmandizing, and suppression of menses (a litany of illness or a recipe for one hell of a weekend?).

At all times in its history, however, a significant number of inmates at Central State Hospital suffered from *general paresis,* a form of dementia caused by untreated syphilis. A mental disease with clear origins in a physical illness, paresis was a natural test case for psychopathology.

Meet the Great Imitator

Before the advent of AIDS, syphilis was the most feared sexually transmitted disease. In its advanced stages, syphilis can cause horrifically disfiguring skin growths, called *gummas,* which blanket the face and torso with hideous, warty lesions. Syphilis can also attack the heart, liver, and brain. In the very worst cases, the disease leaves its host paralyzed, blind, and raving. In the nineteenth and early twentieth centuries, general paresis, caused by advanced syphilis, accounted for a significant proportion of mental health cases.

Although cases may have been diagnosed as far back as classical antiquity, the first major syphilis outbreak in Europe occurred at the close of the fifteenth century. The Germans, who thought the plague had been brought back from the New World, blamed Columbus's patrons by dubbing it the *Spanish disease*; the Spanish shifted the blame onto the French, who, in turn, said they had contracted the *Italian disease* when they were besieging the city of Naples.

It was an Italian, a Veronese physician named Girolamo Fracastoro, who broke this circular firing squad by coining a name for the disease that all of Christendom could agree on.

Published in 1530, *Syphilis siue morbus Gallicus* (*Syphilis, or the French Disease*) is one of the odder medical textbooks you could ever read. It is fifty pages of Latin poetry—1,300 lines of heroic hexameter (which, by the way, doesn't rhyme, but instead takes on this rhythm: *BUM pa-pa, BUM pa-pa, BUM. Pause. Pa-pa, BUM pa-pa, BUM pap-pa, BUM BUM*)—verses that contain a mash-up of medical observation, folk remedies, and deliberate mythmaking in the form of a fantastical/allegorical account of the origin of the disease and its first victim, an unfortunate named *Syphilis*. (This is probably a nod to *Sipylus*, a minor character in Ovid's first century BCE poetical masterwork, *The Metamorphosis,* who appears just long enough to be gruesomely dispatched by Apollo, god of disease.)

Fracastoro is one of those individuals who restores meaning to the overused term *Renaissance man*. He knew a thing or two about astronomy, collected fossils, wrote about philosophy, came up with the idea that diseases were spread by spores (a theory that remained popular right up to the discovery of germs three hundred years later), and was physician not just to a pope, but, for a time, to the entire Council of Trent.

Despite his impressive résumé, *Dottore* Fracastoro could offer little medical insight into syphilis or relief from its symptoms. The best he could do was to recommend **mercury treatments**, which were painful and dangerous, and only marginally effective. Though, to Fracastoro's credit, mercury was the best anyone could do, until the advent of Salvarsan in 1909 and, finally, penicillin in the 1940s.

In 1905, a pair of micropathologists in Berlin, Fritz Schaudinn and Erich Hoffmann, identified the cause of syphilis as a corkscrew-shaped, or *spirochete,* bacterium named *Treponema pallidum* (which is a Greek noun and a Latin adjective that together mean *pale twisted-thread*).

Syphilis develops in three stages, in a process that can take decades to complete. It can attack both the inside and the outside of the body and presents so many possible symptoms that doctors have nicknamed it the Great Imitator. Anywhere from a quarter to a third of people with untreated syphilis develop neurosyphilis, the degenerative nerve disease that causes general paresis.

Boom to Bust

It is in the pathology room where visitors to the Indiana Museum of Medical History can get a more vivid picture of the work that went on in the Old Pathology Building. The glory days of gross pathology cabinets may have been over, but the doctors at Central State were still collecting medically interesting specimens, just on a smaller scale. And, as their living database of prospective specimens, they had all the inmates of the asylum to choose from.

The museum owns some four hundred pathological samples, many of which are on display, including partial and whole brains harvested from former patients of Central State. Some show brain trauma from physical injuries, like being kicked by horses or banging their head into doors, while others bear signs of neurological diseases, such as Alzheimer's and general paresis.

Paresis was a speciality of Dr. Walter Bruetsch, who ran a series of experiments at Central State in the 1920s and 1930s on the so-called malarial cure for syphilis. This quixotic treatment, discovered during the First World War, consisted of deliberately infecting a patient with malaria, which somehow inhibited the syphilis spirochete. Once the syphilis went into remission, the malaria fever would then be cured by administering quinine. More dangerous and uncomfortable than the mercury treatment, the malaria cure offered relief that was nearly as fleeting, because the syphilis would inevitably re-emerge.

It was Dr. Bruetsch who discovered the source of the malaria cure's effectiveness: The white blood cells that attacked malaria also killed the syphilis spirochete. Unfortunately, once the malaria was gone, white blood cell production ceased and the syphilis would return. Before Bruetsch could find any practical application for his research, it was discovered that penicillin would permanently cure syphilis. Overnight, Bruetsch's work became medically irrelevant.

Impressive as the laboratories were at Central State, in the end absolutely nothing came of the psychopathological research conducted there. In the first decades of the twentieth century, medical fashion turned again. Newly developed tranquilizers allowed physicians to deaden the most disruptive symptoms of mental ill-ness, and, *psychotherapy*—the talking cure—began to gain ground on psychopathology. Pioneered by the Viennese physician Sigmund Freud, psychotherapy posited that the cause of most mental illness was emotional trauma rather than physical injury or disease, and that, therefore, looking for surgical or medical cures was to fundamentally misunderstand the nature of the disease.

The psychopathology pioneered at Central State may have been a medical dead end, but in the sweep of history the doctors who labored there and at similar institutions nevertheless made a major contribution to the treatment of mental illness: By redefining insanity as a mental *illness* and not a moral failing or a symptom of demonic possession, as it had been regarded for centuries before, these scientists pointed the way to humane and effective treatment.

Central State was shut down almost twenty years ago, and, except for the Old Pathology Building, almost all its buildings have been demolished. But it might not yet be time to close books on Central State or psychopathology. Since 2010, the institution's pathological samples have moved out of retirement, as researchers at Indiana University have been extracting DNA samples to see if these century-old specimens can help generate a genetic profile for illnesses such as depression or bipolar disorder.

Fashion continues to move, and *micro* has gone *molecular*.

The Indiana Medical History Museum is open to the public from Thursday through Saturday. General admission is $5. For more information, go to **www.imhm.org**.

See also:

Army Field Museum: National Museum of Health and Medicine, Washington, D.C.

Ohio

One Hour with Venus, a Lifetime with Mercury

WHAT: Dough-Boy Prophylactic disposable urethral irrigators

WHERE: Dittrick Museum, Case Western Reserve University, Cleveland

In the waning days of the nineteenth century, the members of the Cleveland Medical Library Association had the foresight to recognize that they were living through a sea change in their profession. Breakthroughs in disease theory, molecular biology, and antiseptics were revolutionizing the way medicine was understood and practiced. The leeches and lancets, the pewter enema syringes and portable amputation kits they had trained on were on the way out and would soon be nothing more than half-remembered medical oddities. So in 1898, they created a museum to preserve that history.

More than one century, one change of venue, and several changes of name later, the Dittrick Medical History Center at Case Western Reserve University continues to carry on that project. Housed in the College of Arts and Sciences, it is not just an active medical resource; the center also functions as a sort of meta-museum that attempts to put medical history into a larger historical context. The curators' intention is to demonstrate how even something as putatively neutral and objective as science has real consequences in other realms of human activity and is itself not immune to the historical forces at play around it.

Nothing illustrates the museum's purpose better than its latest acquisition, the Percy Skuy Collection on the History of Contraception. Mr. Skuy, onetime president of Canadian contraceptive maker Ortho Pharmaceutical, assembled a private collection of more than 650 historical contraceptive devices. Under the care of the Dittrick Museum, the collection has doubled, making it the world's largest and most comprehensive exhibit on birth control.

It's difficult not to snicker at the idea of a contraceptive museum—and that reaction is exactly what the museum curators would like you to think about.

Sexuality is an eternal flashpoint in American culture. As the contraceptive collection shows, sex has always been a fiercely contested issue, where medicine, law, public morality, and personal freedom dogpile all over each other in an ungainly struggle for dominance. The history of sex is the history of all these threads and the strange and sometimes fleeting alliances among them.

Skuy's Follies

Ever since humans first understood the connection between sexual activity and pregnancy, they have gone to absurd lengths to enjoy the former while avoiding the latter. From the pragmatically inspired but actually useless and uncomfortable candy-bar-wrapper condom to the metaphysically justified (at least to the ancient Egyptians) but unappealing Nile crocodile dung, to the just-plain-wrong Chinese beaver-testicle tea, you can find in the Skuy Collection a panoply of historic contraceptives and prophylactics, both effective and not-so-effective.

One of the more disturbing items on the shelves of the Skuy Collection comes in an innocuous package. Standard issue for every American soldier in the early twentieth century, this small, white-and-orange cardboard packet is emblazoned with eye-pleasing black block lettering that reads *Dough-Boy Prophylactic* and frames an illustration of a First World War soldier, tin hat jauntily askew and bayonetted rifle at the ready. The contents are five small rubber tubes, rifle shaped with a thick rectangular base and an ominously long, skinny barrel, and each loaded with a 1.5-ounce dose of calomel ointment; a small cotton sack; and a sheet of highly euphemistic directions.

After sexual intercourse—so the directions direct—the soldier is to take one of the tubes—or *urethral syringes*—and insert the tip fully into "the canal," squeezing gently while withdrawing. He then should coat his virile part with the remainder of the ointment, sheath the old fellow in the stain-resistant cotton sack, and allow it to rest for twelve hours.

The painful stinging is a sign the treatment is working. So is the intensive perspiration.

Calomel, for us non-chemists, is another name for *mercury chloride*. Yes, *that* mercury, the silvery stuff in thermometers you're not supposed to touch and the poisonous stuff in fish you're not supposed to eat. Low doses of this caustic heavy metal cause hyper-salivation and perspiration. A little bit more, and you'll get a ferociously upset stomach. More still and your hair and teeth will fall out. Take small doses over a long time, and you might get any of a smorgasbord of symptoms: numbness, impaired vision, slurred speech, hallucinations, mood disorders, tremors, paralysis.

Mercury is terrible stuff, but for centuries it was the primary line of defense against something even more terrible: **syphilis.** This historic scourge begins by causing lesions and flu-like symptoms in its host, but, if left untreated, can lead to disfigurement, nerve damage, blindness, madness, and paralysis.

Strangely enough, if applied soon after exposure, mercury *can* prevent a syphilis infection. (The delicate syphilis spirochete is no match for the corrosive heavy metal.) If that initial treatment fails, however, subsequent mercury injections can provide some relief from the symptoms. But they are not a cure. Nothing was, until penicillin became widely available in the 1940s. Before then, a syphilis infection could mean a lifetime of painful and harmful treatments that were almost as bad as the disease.

Girolamo Fracastoro, the man who gave the world the name *syphilis*, also published one of the earliest accounts of the mercury treatment in 1530. A man of the world, he knew that no reasonable person would willingly inject mercury up his urethra. So to him, he offered this admonition in Latin verse, which would be echoed by physicians for five hundred years:

His igitur totum oblinere, atque obducere corpus
Ne obscoenum, ne turpe puta: per talia morbus
Tollitur, & nihil esse potest obscoenius ipso.

Which, roughly translated, is:

So over the body spread this and smear,
No matter how shameful or gross it appear;
For through this treatment will come ease,
And nothing is grosser than the disease.

Comstock Laws

Now here's the rub: In 1917, there was another inexpensive, easy-to-use prophylactic that was more effective than calomel and way less gross. It was the rubber condom. Soldiers from every other nation gathered in war-ravaged France carried them as standard issue. But not our doughboys.

Why this was so is entirely the result of Americans' schizophrenic attitude about health and sexuality at the time. *Prophylactics* like calomel were considered respectable medicine, because their job is to protect against disease (*phylax* is Greek for *guardian*). On the other hand, *contraceptives* like condoms, whose primary purpose was to prevent pregnancy (and thereby, it was thought, facilitate irresponsible, consequence-free sexual activity), were, by their very nature, "obscene, lewd, and/or lascivious" devices and, thus, illegal. This casuistry created a counterintuitive legal situation where it was essentially illegal to prevent the *spread* of syphilis but fine to *treat* it after the fact.

The ban on contraceptives was codified in the so-called *Comstock Act,* which Congress passed in 1873, after intense lobbying by a coalition of business and religious leaders fronted by an energetic social reformer named Anthony Comstock. A deliberate attempt to put sexuality in its entirety outside the reach of public discussion, the law banned the possession and distribution of not just pornography and contraceptives but even *information* about contraception. Family planning as we know it today was legally regarded as an unspeakable obscenity.

It is common for anti-pornography movements to claim to be acting on behalf of women, protecting them from exploitation and danger. But Comstock and crew were more worried about protecting the virtue of young men, who, as the growing nation began to industrialize, were leaving the farms in droves. Seeking out opportunity in the cities, they found it in spades: jobs, yes, but also an enticing array of moral hazards—drinking, gambling, cursing, smoking, sexing—activities known collectively then as *the sporting life*. Keeping young men in the office and away from the enervating pursuit of the sporting life was the original purpose of Comstock's moral-reform campaign, which decided that the most efficacious prescription was a large dose of personal responsibility and a touch of the short, sharp shock. The Comstock laws were designed not to lessen social harm, but rather to provide spectacular examples of punishment that would make it clear that those who refused to toe the line would just have to live with the consequences of their iniquitous behavior.

By the early twentieth century, those *consequences* (i.e., sexually transmitted diseases and unwanted pregnancies) were making themselves felt. Under these social strains, some aspects of sexuality started to be reframed in terms of public health rather than morality and personal responsibility.

The first shift came in 1918—the year the First World War ended—when the courts removed condoms from the proscribed list—but only if they were marketed as *prophylactics* and not *contraceptives*. Protection was OK, but, for many Americans, *contraception* was still a dirty word. (Condoms remained in this twilight space until 1938 when, in the awesomely named *United States v. One Package of Japanese Pessaries*, a packet of contraceptive diaphragms defeated the Attorney General's Office, and the Supreme Court lifted the federal ban on contraceptives. But they remained illegal in most states. It was not until 1972 that the Supreme Court found such state-level bans unconstitutional.)

Legalization came too late for our soldiers in France. About one in twenty recruits had joined the army with a venereal disease; one in ten left with one—despite the aid of urethral syringes. The '20s may have roared, but for many they burned. A legacy of painful urethral irrigations and dangerous intramuscular injections taught another generation the expression, *"One hour with Venus and a lifetime with Mercury."*

Access to the Dittrick Museum is by appointment only. Visit the museum's page at **www.cwru.edu/artsci/dittrick/museum** for more information.

See also:

Girolamo Fracastoro, Syphilis: Syphilitic brains, Indiana

THE SOUTHEAST

Kentucky

Frankenstein's Daughter

WHAT: Medical Venus

WHERE: Monroe Moosnick Medical and Science Museum, Transylvania University, Lexington

Founded in 1780, Lexington's Transylvania University actually pre-dates the state of Kentucky by more than a decade. You can save your vampire jokes, because the school takes its name not from Romanian geography, but from the original American settlement around Lexington, which was so named because it was *the region across the forest (trans + silvan + ia)* from western Virginia.

But while the connection between the university and Dracula's Carpathian home may be purely incidental, it is strikingly apposite: Transy U's medical museum, with its outstanding relics of early nineteenth-century medicine, has more than a passing resemblance to a torture chamber from a gothic novel.

But amid the fetus skeletons and the human jawbones, the frightful, archaic tools and the colorful apothecary jars, there is a greater treasure. Transy's Monroe Moosnick museum houses a unique medical object: the nation's only surviving Medical Venus.

Deconstructing Venus

Today she is a drab and disfigured shabby doll. Her arms are lost, and her body is broken off below the hips. Rescued from the 1863 fire that razed the campus, she is smoke damaged and bereft of the protective glass coffin that once encased her. The wax skin that used to cover her face is gone, and now her glass eyes stare out from a knot of striated muscle. In short, she's a wreck. But in her prime, Transy's Medical Venus was a dazzling work of science and art. Cast by master craftsmen from a blend of wax, resin, and pigment, she was painstakingly built up, layer after layer, like a Renaissance oil painting, until her skin glowed with the richness of life. She was a marvel of her kind.

Medical Venuses like the one on display at Transy were teaching tools in the eighteenth and nineteenth centuries, life-sized "dissectible," reusable models that could substitute for actual cadavers, which were difficult, and sometimes illegal, to obtain. They worked just like Russian nesting dolls, whose heads are removed only to reveal smaller dolls inside—except in the Venuses' case, the skin of the torso was removed to expose muscle below, then entrails, heart, lungs, and finally down to the womb with tiny fetus nestled inside.

The example in the Monroe Moosnick was acquired from the waxworks of Florence, which was then producing the best medical wax models in the world. The Florentine *ceroplastica* served primarily the Grand Duke of Tuscany, Peter Leopold von Habsburg-Lothringen (who eventually would become king of Hungary, too, and ruler of the Holy Roman Empire—don't ask:

Italian history is a mess). This aristocrat many times over was also an Enlightenment virtuoso, who invented the public museum in 1775, when he opened a natural history collection known as La Specola (or Observatory). Anyone who wore clean clothes and could pay the modest admission was allowed in—a remarkably democratic idea for the time. At its unveiling, La Specola boasted nineteen full anatomical figures plus 1,400 organs and body parts, all exquisitely crafted from wax.

The displays at La Specola were made in close collaboration between anatomists, who dissected corpses, and sculptors, who meticulously modeled the body parts in clay. It took two hundred cadavers to supply all the parts for a single full-body mold. When the wax casts were done, artists would embellish them by hand. They painted in details, used dyed thread to simulate veins, and varnished surfaces to give them a natural, slimy sheen.

Being artists, they also couldn't help but editorialize. These master craftsmen didn't want their creations to be just generic anatomical ciphers, they wanted them to be perfection incarnate—perfectly articulated organs within and perfectly idealized femininity without. They gave their models flowing hair, and adorned them with jewelry and other feminine finery. One aspect of these Venuses that has particularly fascinated and troubled later generations of philosophers and art historians is the way they are posed. The models lie on their backs, but not the way a cadaver does, stiff and heavy and dead. The Venuses' limbs are lithe, their bodies arranged in lively contrapposto, and faces rendered with rapturous expressions that suggest both ecstasy and torment.

There is room for an allegorical interpretation that takes these models as a stand-in for Nature, seductively beckoning the naturalist, who unveils Her mysteries, one after the other, until his inquisitive hands have despoiled Her of all secrets.

Anatomical, allegorical, or straight-up kinky, the effect of seeing one of these supine Venuses in action—knees bent in a fruitless gesture of modesty, head turned demurely away, lips frozen in the act of mouthing what might be a groan or could be a sigh—while layer after layer of spectacular viscera is removed and set aside . . . well, it's disconcerting.

It was Dr. Charles Caldwell who commissioned the Medical Venus. This talented, if charmless, pupil of **Dr. Benjamin Rush** had reorganized Transy's medical school, turning it into a solid modern institution. In reward, the university sent him to Europe in 1821 with $1,500 and instructions to procure everything that a top medical training program needed. When the Venus was delivered in 1823, the Lexington newspapers thought it worthy of reporting. They found her beauty both *charming* and *arresting*.

Although she was absolutely state-of-the-art, the Medical Venus's days were numbered. Her arrival heightened debate within the medical school over the role of **gross dissection** in education, with the more forward-looking members insisting on using real and not simulated human bodies in the classroom. Tensions grew so strong that, in 1837, half of Transy's instructors defected to start a school of their own in Louisville, where it was easier to get access to cadavers. Ironically, it was Dr. Caldwell himself who led the faction.

The Monroe Moosnick Medical and Science Museum is open by appointment only.

See also:
Benjamin Rush, Lewis and Clark's latrines, Montana

Gross dissection: Cemetery gun, Pennsylvania; Syphilitic brains, Indiana

"There Is No Reason Women Should Not Bear Spaying as Well as Other Animals"
—John Hunter, the father of modern surgery

WHAT: McDowell House, Apothecary, and Gardens, site of the first ovariotomy

WHERE: Danville

One of the easiest dates to remember in all of history is Christmas Day, 800—the day an upstart barbarian king named Charlemagne was anointed Emperor of the Romans. Politically and psychologically, it was a watershed moment that ended nearly two millennia of Greco-Roman supremacy and midwifed modern Europe.

Exactly one thousand and nine years later, a country doctor named Ephraim McDowell became the first person to successfully remove an ovarian tumor, and on Christmas Day, 1809, in a scrappy, up-and-coming corner of the English-speaking world, the practice of abdominal surgery was born.

Alas, the history-making tumor is gone, but Dr. McDowell's house remains, and it is now a museum. Guided tours lead visitors through the meticulously restored house and apothecary—a trim, two-story box that is an almost painfully pure example of Colonial architecture, right down to its white clapboard siding and green shutters and door. It even has a white picket fence.

It was in an upstairs bedroom that Dr. McDowell removed a

twenty-two-and-a-half-pound tumor from the abdomen of Mrs. Jane Crawford, without the comfort of anesthesia or the protection of antiseptics—neither of which were known of at the time. To ease the pain, Mrs. Crawford sang psalms and recited Bible passages. The operation took 25 minutes.

The Saga of Surgery

Today's surgeons may see themselves as the top guns of the medical profession, but it wasn't so long ago that they were considered its bottom feeders.

Between the twin dangers of shock and infection—a medical Scylla and Charybdis that would not be easily negotiated until late in the nineteenth century—there was not an awful lot that early surgeons could do without killing their patients. So that was one strike against the profession.

Strike two was the surgeons themselves. In the Middle Ages, when the Church oversaw the universities, earning a degree automatically admitted a graduate into the lower orders of clergy. Since holy people were forbidden to shed blood, surgery was delegated to barbers, who may not have known much anatomy but were very deft with a knife. And so a division of labor was established: Physicians diagnosed, while uneducated barber-surgeons did all the dirty work.

And that leads to strike number three: Surgery was despised because it was an applied art. Serious intellectuals were gentlemen who studied ancient authorities, like **Galen** and Aristotle, and worked in the clear and ennobling medium of philosophy using the tools of logic. *Actual* bodies were messy, déclassé things, and studying them directly, it was believed, would only get you lost in the weeds.

On the spectrum of respectable careers, then, surgery was a shutout. *"Make something of your life"* was the advice an aspiring medieval doctor might have heard as he was packing to leave for college. *"Get that philosophy degree; you don't want to end up a bum like that drunk down the street, the surgeon."*

During the Renaissance, the status of the human body—and consequently that of surgery—began to change. While medievals tended to see themselves as condemned to living encased in flesh-sacks of frailty and sin, a younger generation of artists and intellectuals regarded the body as a miraculous machine. Getting up close to it—studying its joints, its bones, its muscles and even cutting it open to see how it worked—was, for them, something not at all dirty or morbid; it was an act of praise for the divine intelligence that they believed was the Author of humankind and all of nature.

As early natural philosophers, like Leonardo da Vinci and Francis Bacon and dozens of lesser known pioneers, gradually pieced together the scientific method, empirical observation became not just accepted but finally celebrated in the intellectual community. By the mid-eighteenth century, dissection had become a standard part of medical education, and the wall of snobbery between physicians and surgeons started to erode.

By the end of the 1700s, the first generation of surgeons was emerging whose thorough knowledge of anatomy and meticulous attention to technique could compensate, at least to a degree, for the otherwise vast deficiencies of their time. It was a moment of intellectual vigor and daring, when men of science were prepared to stake audacious wagers to plunder nature's secrets. It was the **Age of Heroic Medicine**.

An exemplar of the era was Scottish anatomist **John Hunter**, the father of modern surgery. A man of boundless curiosity and scrupulous observation, he conducted sometimes ghastly experiments with a *what-the-hell?* sense of gusto and adventure: like when he grafted teeth onto a chicken's head to see if they would take root. (Improbably enough, they did.) He also transplanted a rooster's penis onto a hen's head. (It did not work.) But Hunter held no special animus toward chickens. He experimented frequently on dogs and pigs. Once, with the permission of King George II himself, he perfected his technique of tying off arterial aneurysms by practicing on a full-grown stag from the royal parkland.

Nor was Hunter himself above taking one for team Natural History: He was perfectly willing to be his own guinea pig, especially in his more ethically questionable experiments—such as the time he exposed himself to gonorrhea just to see if he would contract syphilis—by applying infected pus obtained from a patient to his own penis. (Hunter, like many of his contemporaries, mistakenly believed that gonorrhea and syphilis were the same disease.)

Prickly and profane, Hunter embodied a peculiarly Enlightenment style of genius, in which was combined an obsessive curiosity, a chilling degree of intellectual detachment balanced by an unexpected and deep compassion, and an ironic—even cynical—sensibility that leveled all mundane human concerns to triviality. The whole is a weirdly attractive if slightly monstrous personality. Only an Enlightenment thinker, for instance, could have formulated such a well-intentioned, droll, and utterly offensive statement as the epigram that starts this entry. The brusque tone of the quotation, which comes from a lecture of 1786, overshadows its radical message: that performing a human

ovariotomy was, in theory, no more complicated than the unremarkable event of spaying a barnyard animal.

Having laid out the case for ovarian surgery, however, Hunter
would die without attempting one. That role in history would be
claimed by a semi-credentialed country doctor in the newly liberated American colonies.

Passing the Flame of Knowledge

Trained in the late eighteenth century, Ephraim McDowell was
steeped in the forward-leaning spirit of his age. He studied in
Edinburgh, a world-class intellectual hub at the time that rivaled
London. Hints of the friction that would soon erupt into the
Napoleonic Wars, however, compelled him to cut short his train-
ing, and he returned home without a degree.

But lack of a diploma did not stop McDowell from setting
up shop back in his native Kentucky, where he soon gained the
reputation as the best doctor west of the Alleghenies—which is
why he was called in to consult on the case of Mrs. Crawford, a
forty-something mother of five whose new set of twins were well
past due.

A quick exam convinced McDowell that Mrs. Crawford's
"twins" were in fact a massive ovarian tumor. As a student back
in Edinburgh, he had heard lectures from John Hunter's disciples on the theoretical possibility of removing such growths.
But many other physicians thought that the practical barriers
were insurmountable—even if the patient survived the shock
and the blood loss of the operation, the abdomen was particularly vulnerable to infection, and, in a time before antibiotics,
there was no cure for that. Puncturing the *peritoneum*, the sac

that protects the internal organs, was widely believed to be a death sentence.

You can practically see the gears turning in his mind when McDowell laid out his gambit. Very gently he told Mrs. Crawford that there was no medicine that could fix her ailment. The tumor would continue to grow until it eventually killed her. Painfully. Agonizingly, in fact.

Her only chance was to have it removed.

Of course, McDowell candidly confessed, he had never removed one. But neither had anyone else. Besides, it wasn't as if she was going to find a better trained surgeon here on the margins of the civilized world.

Nevertheless, the choice was hers: a lingering, miserable death, or . . . a straw of hope.

Eleven days later, Mrs. Crawford appeared on his doorstep. She and her twenty-two-pound tumor had made the 60-mile trip from their home in Motley's Glen, on horseback, in the freeze of a late December.

The surgeon wasted no time. According to McDowell's notes, he penned a prayer before he started the operation. He then removed his coat, and had his assistants hold the patient down. It is not recorded whether she was offered the small mercy of laudanum drops or spiced rum, which represent the gamut of painkillers available at the time, but her surgeon did show her the courtesy at the end of the procedure of washing her intestines thoroughly before tucking them back away and sewing her up.

It is probably McDowell's attention to cleanliness that saved his patient's life. That and Mrs. Crawford's frontier grit. Five days after the operation, McDowell found his patient on her feet and making her bed. After twenty-five days of recovery, she rode the 60 miles back home.

McDowell's life-saving intervention was no fluke. He repeated the procedure thirteen times with only four fatalities. But when he was ready to go public with his breakthrough in 1817, he had difficultly finding a publisher. And when he finally did, Mc-Dowell's claims were met not with professional skepticism but virulent incredulity. The British medical community was not receptive to being bested by a former colony, and it took almost a decade for McDowell to receive his due credit. But when vindication did come in 1826, it arrived in this satisfyingly abject and public apology from a leading British medical journal, *The Medical and Chirurgical Review*:

> A back settlement of America—Kentucky, has beaten the mother country, nay, Europe itself, with all the boasted surgeons thereof, in the fearful and formidable operation of gastrotomy with extraction of diseased ovaries . . . There were circumstances in the narrative of some of the first three cases, that caused misgivings in our minds, for which uncharitableness we ask pardon of God and Dr. McDowell of Danville.

In 1823, McDowell was awarded an honorary medical degree from the University of Maryland, the only degree he would ever receive. Dr. McDowell died in 1830, at the age of 59. Ironically, what did him in was probably peritonitis from a burst appendix.

Mrs. Crawford outlived her doctor by twelve years, dying in 1842, at age seventy-nine.

The McDowell house and garden is open seven days a week,

most months of the year. Admission is $7 for adults and $2 for children. For more information, go to **www.mcdowellhouse .com.**

See also:

Galen, Age of Heroic Medicine: Lewis and Clark's latrines, Montana

John Hunter: Cemetery gun, Pennsylvania

Tennessee

Doing It for Conservation

WHAT: Behind the scenes at the herpetology exhibit

WHERE: Nashville Zoo at Grassmere, Nashville

For those of us not lucky enough to captain a Fortune 500 company, own a vineyard, or participate in the professional snowboard circuit, the unavoidable cocktail-party question *"So, what do you do?"* is not always a welcome one. But at least you can be thankful that you don't have to answer, *"I masturbate reptiles."*

Save the Snot Otter

North America's largest salamander is in peril. Topping out at three feet long, this holdover from the dinosaur age is called

A snot otter salamander

snot otter by some. Others prefer *devil dog*. But the name that you will see most often for *Cryptobranchus alleganiensis* is *hellbender*—a ferocious moniker indeed, but one that this gentle giant, with its stubby four-fingered limbs, tiny button eyes, and wide-grinning mouth, decidedly does *not* live up to.

For millions of years, hellbenders have crawled sluggishly over the rocky bottoms of Appalachian rivers and streams, searching for crayfish to munch. At their peak, you could find hellbenders in fourteen southern and eastern states. But over the past twenty or thirty years, the population has declined by almost 90 percent. For reasons unknown, the hellbender has simply stopped breeding.

Perhaps environmental changes are killing their eggs. Or maybe pollution absorbed through the salamander's thin, permeable skin is rendering them sterile. Whatever the cause, the hellbender is dying out in the wild.

Are You a Cryopreservationist, or Are Your Hands Just Cold?

But where nature fails, science steps in—with a phalanx of animal fluffers. An international research team is trying to save the hellbender through a technique called *cryopreservation*. A branch of *cryonics*, the science of freezing and then reviving living tissue, cryopreservation is a proposed means of saving endangered animals by freezing their sperm, in hopes of someday artificially breeding the species and releasing it back into the wild.

The team has successfully revived hellbender sperm that was frozen for six months, which is a hopeful start. But it is only a first step.

In order to continue conducting their deep-freeze experiments on hellbender sperm researchers need a steady supply of the stuff. Collecting it is a task that has fallen to veterinarians at the Nashville zoo. There is no high-tech cheat: The vets have to go at it by hand, "milking" the salamanders by rubbing a finger between the front legs and tail.

It's a good thing for them that hellbenders are easygoing, tractable beasts—or, as one researcher puts it, somewhat distastefully in this context, "big, flaccid creatures." You don't want to imagine the mischief that a yard-long, slippery salamander could get up to when sufficiently aroused.

See also:
Cryonics: Frozen Dead Guy Days, Colorado

Alabama

Twinkle, Twinkle, Little Worms

WHAT: Dismalite glowworms

WHERE: Dismals Canyon, Phil Campbell

What long-since-forgotten outrage could have driven some anonymous, but clearly dyspeptic, Scots-Irish frontiersman to christen this lush and colorful canyon in northwestern Alabama "the Dismals"? Perhaps it was the impossibility of obtaining a decent haggis anywhere for miles around.

Apt or not, the name has endured in this area, which now comprises 85 acres of privately owned parkland at the southernmost end of the Cumberland Plateau. With campgrounds and rental cabins, and the requisite attractions of swimming, hiking, and waterfall admiring, Dismals Canyon is not unlike a thousand other campsites dotting the Appalachians. However, at night this mask of uniformity falls away, and the glowing heart of Dismals Canyon is revealed—its eerie, glowing, pulsating, bioluminescent heart.

Some dark summer evening, if you can find the courage, descend the old wooden stairs that lead to the bottom of this sandstone gorge in Franklin County, cross the ominous swing bridge with its clanky chain handrail, and, standing before the craggy hollow known as Witches Cavern, slick with moss and slimy algae, extinguish your flashlight. This will be your reward: Once your eyes adjust to the near total darkness, you will see a constellation of unearthly blue lights that stretch up the canyon walls until they merge with the silvery stars above. If you look closely enough, you will notice the cave-side constellations twitching and slowly changing shape. . . .

Dismals Canyon is home to the largest known concentration of a rare species of glowworm unique to North America. The people associated with Dismals Canyon like to call these luminescent worms *dismalites*; individuals with no particular interest in branding these insects, however, call them the larvae of *Orfelia fultoni*, or, more colloquially, *baby fungus gnats*.

Adult *O. fultani* are tiny, mosquito-like bugs that look like any other gnat (of which there are hundreds and hundreds of nearly identical species). It is only the larval *O. fultani* that glow, and they have the further distinction of generating the bluest light of any glowworm. And they are found only one place on earth, right here in the US of A.

A Glowing Personality

The quality of generating one's own light from one's own body is called *bioluminescence,* from a Greek word meaning *life* and a Latin word meaning *light*. On land, bioluminescence is rare, the most well-known exemplars being glowworms (which are actually not worms at all but the wormlike larvae and adult females of a family of beetles called *Phengodidae*), and fireflies, also known as *Lampyridae*.

Ocean creatures, on the other hand, are masters of biolumi-nescence. From the expressively scintillating skin of the squid to the dangling headlamp of the monstrous angler fish to the serene reefs of certain varieties of coral, the ocean is practically shimmering with bioluminosity. It is estimated that 90 percent of deep-sea creatures have some form of bioluminescence. There are also some species of fungus and microorganisms that make their own light.

Bioluminescence happens when a chemical pigment called a *luciferin* and a catalyst called a *lucifrase* combine and oxidize. (The root word in each—*luc*—is another Latin word for *light*, and, yes, it is also the root in the diabolical cognomen *Lucifer*, which means *Light-carrier*.) There are many varieties of luciferin and lucifrase, which accounts for the variation in bioluminescent light, from the red glow of the deep-swimming black dragonfish to the yellow-green of fireflies to the cool blue of *O. fultoni*.

(In case you are wondering, bioluminescence is not combus-tion. It is perfectly harmless, and animals that possess this trait have no special resistance to heat. Unlike, say, an old-fashioned incandescent lightbulb, bioluminescence generates light but al-most no heat. Less heat means less wasted energy, and that's one reason scientists have studied this phenomenon. Another rea-son is that researchers are learning how to use biolumines-cence to mark genetically modified cells; the glowing makes it much easier to track these special cells when they mix with or-dinary ones.)

Conscientious conservers of energy, dismalites glow only at night. If you happen upon one by day, you will see simply a quarter-inch-long gelatinous blob, translucent milky white in color with black flecks, that looks exactly like a French vanilla

Gummi Worm (if such a thing exists). The black flecks are the larva's chemical "lamps," which are visible through its pallid sides.

But looks aren't the only unpleasant part about these luminescent maggots. Dismalites hunt by extruding a stringy, sticky substance from their mouths, which they drape haphazardly around their lairs like messy spiderwebs. These webs are infused with oxalic acid (aka rust cleaner), which, it is speculated, acts as a sort of pre-digester for any creature unfortunate enough to get entangled in the caustic strands. Once the prey has been thoroughly stuck, the victorious dismalite gloatingly crawls out to further torment its helpless captive. Springing like a self-styled cobra, the tiny larva will strike from time to time. It is conjectured that this is the dismalite's way of injecting more oxalic acid to further soften up its meal.

Most entomologists think that the purpose of the dismalites' glow is to attract prey, such as moths and other flying insects that are drawn to light. Another theory is that the bioluminescence acts as a warning to would-be predators that gobbling up a dismalite will also get them a mouthful of nasty, acid-doused web. Maybe both are true.

You can visit Dismals Canyon on a nighttime glowworm hunt. The tour schedule varies with the season and glowworm activity, so check Dismals Canyon page for the latest updates: **www .dismalscanyon.com**.

Louisiana

These Totally Suck

WHAT: Lead nipple shields

WHERE: The New Orleans Pharmacy
Museum, New Orleans

In 1803, when President Thomas Jefferson purchased what is now roughly the middle third of the nation, he paid the French just over $11 million and forgave almost another $4 million of their debts. He did this primarily to get his hands on New Orleans.

Of course, the port of New Orleans controlled trade up the Mississippi River and might have been used by hostile nations as a base from which to harass the western flank of the United States. But is it too much to hope that savory gumbo, sugary beignets, or a potent regional cocktail called the *sazerac* might have swayed the president's decision?

From its earliest days, New Orleans has been synonymous with *joie de vivre*. After two centuries' assimilation into the US, and having weathered some infamously difficult times recently, the city's French heart is still beating strong—and, to the detriment of this book, its soul remains Gallic enough to eschew anything as gauche and unlovely as the gross.

Home of the jazz funeral and host to voodoo shops and guided cemetery tours, the Crescent City abounds in attractions that in any other place would be treasure troves of morbidity. But here, amid the cobbled streets and the elegant wrought-iron railings of the French Quarter, the garish intensity of any local grotesquery is softened by a romantic gauze—just as, when seen through the filter of a Stevie Nicks shawl draped over a vintage Tiffany lamp, even the hideous glare of a fluorescent lightbulb in a dorm room can appear as lush and inviting as the glow of any Parisian bordello.

But what book of curious Americana could be complete without any mention of New Orleans? So here is one attraction that combines a measure of history, a dash of sophistication, and a large slice of weirdness.

The New Orleans Pharmacy Museum is located in the old shop of Louis Joseph Dufilho, Jr., who, according to the museum, was the nation's first licensed pharmacist. Dufilho's old pharmacy now houses a great collection of antique pharmaceuticals and medical tools, all set out as if they were part of a working nineteenth-century apothecary. Ornate mahogany shelves line the walls from floor to ceiling and are stocked with all the requisite fluids, pills, and powders. Glass-fronted cases of even more ornate mahogany display antique medical instruments and quack gadgets—syringes, tweezers, urethral irrigators, eyeglasses, lancets. Beside the antique brass cash register sits a white pot that looks just like a soup tureen, except for the fact that stenciled on its side in big black letters is the word *leeches*—the early

nineteenth-century physician's cure for any malady caused by an
excess of blood. (We all know how having *too* much blood can be
such a nuisance!)

American pharmacists of Dufilho's time would have practiced
European medicine, with a sprinkling of Native American and
African herbalism, so among the opium concoctions and creams
of arsenic and mercury—which represented state-of-the-art European medicine—you can also spot voodoo preparations, like
love potions.

A more unusual and spectacular display is a soda fountain
from the 1830s. Although it is identified most strongly with the
first half of the twentieth century, the drugstore soda bar—that
universal after-school hangout where teenagers in poodle skirts
or letterman jackets drank hand-mixed colas or chocolate malts
and idled away the hours in the days before enclosed shopping
malls and coffeehouse chains—had a medical origin. Since many
of their concoctions tasted simply awful, pharmacists learned to
mix sweetened and flavored syrups with carbonated water to
help patients wash down their bitter medicines. Some of these
potions were sold as patent medicines of their own, which is
how Coca-Cola got its start. (Of course, back in its earliest
days, when it was known as *Pemberton's French Wine Coca*, the
beverage was mostly cocaine-infused bordeaux with a touch of
stimulant cola nut, so it did contain a strong dose of, shall we say,
active ingredients.)

When our nation was still young, professional credentialing
was more fluid all around. It was not unusual, for example, for
physicians and surgeons to practice with spurious degrees or
none at all. While most local jurisdictions did have guidelines
for pharmacists, they tended to be weak and laxly enforced. At
the federal level, there was hardly any pharmaceutical regulation

at all until Congress passed the Pure Food and Drug Act of 1906. It is no accident, then, that the snake-oil salesman of the traveling medicine show is such an enduring image of the great American flimflam artist.

In 1804, the state of Louisiana took the lead in regulation by establishing an official druggist licensing board, which was composed of pharmacists and physicians who administered a three-hour certifying examination. It was twelve years before they had any takers, but in 1816 Louis Joseph Dufilho, Jr., sat for and passed his exams.

In 1823, America's first bona fide pharmacist opened shop at a newly built townhouse on Chartres Street. Under various managements, the location remained a pharmacy for about fifty years. After housing several other businesses, the building fell into disrepair. Eventually it ended up in the hands of the city, which intended to reopen it as a Napoleon museum. Evidently, the site of Dufilho's pharmacy had been mistaken for the Girod House, the home of a former New Orleans mayor, Nicholas Girod, who purportedly had offered his residence to Napoleon Bonaparte when the military genius and onetime emperor of France was a down-on-his-luck exile on the tiny island of Saint Helena.

When the city fathers were informed of their mistake, they dug a little deeper and found out about Dufilho. That was good enough for them, and in 1950 the New Orleans Pharmacy Museum opened its doors for the first time.

Mother's Little Helpers

Among the colorful jars and exotic potions on the shelves of the Pharmacy Museum, it is easy to miss one small item of rightfully forgotten medicine: two 3-inch disks of smooth gray metal shaped like tiny dented and battered sombreros. The purpose of these devices, made from an alloy of tin and lead, was to protect the sore, overworked nipples of nursing mothers.

On the scale of medical-implement horrors, you might think that nipple shields rate rather low. If so, then you obviously have not sufficiently considered the nightmare that is nursing a baby human being. On top of the hormonal adjustments and the bodily transformations and the chronic, sanity-abolishing sleep deprivation that accompany ushering a child into the world, nursing new mothers must also endure the humiliation of being reduced to a mobile feeding station on call every two hours.

All that chewing and suckling eight times a day and the alternation from moist to dry to moist again can cause a chafing and irritation that can hardly be conveyed by the mere words *chafing* and *irritation*. An advertisement for nipple shields from a 1913 issue of the *American Journal of Nursing* called nursing "the most exquisite agony in the world."

Not that the makers of the nipple shield had that much sympathy for the suffering of mothers *per se*, for the ad continues that, once a woman "has nobly done her duty to her husband and to the state, her sufferings should be minimized, *in order to induce her to continue*."

Do you hear that, mothers? Sure, we gentlemen understand your situation and would like to ease your suffering, but what's in it for the state?

Worn against the skin between nursings, the nipple shields prevented chafing against clothing. Since they were not perforated, they could not be worn while nursing and were not intended to protect against the gnashing gums of a famished infant. The manufacturers did, however, advertise that their shields possessed the medical power to sooth sore nipples—a claim that is sort of true. Trapped between the lead shield and the mother's warm skin, residual breast milk could slightly sour and react with the metallic crown, which would yield an infinitesimal amount of lead lactate, a mild, soothing astringent.

From the mother's perspective, then, nipple shields were reasonably effective, or at least better than nothing. But from the baby's point of view, there was a problem. Lead poisons our organs, it weakens bones, and inhibits the development of nerves. It is particularly harmful to developing children.

The minuscule amount of lead that could be absorbed from the shields was negligible to the mother but not so for the tiny infant at her breast. In the 1940s, amid fears of possible poisoning, lead nipple shields were withdrawn from the market.

Way to ruin it for Mom again, kids!

The New Orleans Pharmacy Museum is open Tuesday through Sunday. Adult admission is $5, and kids are free. Go to **www** **.pharmacymuseum.org** for more information.

Florida

How to Charm a Worm

WHAT: The Worm Gruntin' Festival

WHERE: Sopchoppy

Two men engaging in the fine art of worm gruntin'

Doesn't it seem like there's never a worm around when you really need one? Well, in the swampy South, there is a group of talented individuals who could teach you a trick that would leave you never wanting for worms again.

It's called *worm gruntin'* but, contrary to what you might think, these grunters don't go around snorting like pigs. Here's what they do: First, the intrepid worm hunters locate a promising patch of soft, moist ground—just the sort of home that worms find irresistible. Next, they hammer a long wooden stake into the soil. This is called a *stob*, and across its top is drawn a dull saw blade or long metal file called an *iron*. This rubbing produces a deep stuttering sound like rasping, croaking . . . or *grunting*.

That's where the skill comes in. Most people can scrape away all day on a stob and get nothing more than a sore arm. But a skilled grunter knows how to hit just the right note that will lure all the nearby worms out of their subterranean lairs. Once the ground is a-wiggle with squirming creepy-crawlies, the grunter grabs them by the handful and drops them into buckets to be sold as fish bait.

The Apalachicola National Forest, in Florida's panhandle, is a hotspot for worm gruntin'. The forest is home to a species of worm that is especially prized for fishing. *Diplocardia mississippiensis* is much fatter than the skinny, red earthworms you're probably used to seeing in your lawn. It gets its name—*double-hearted from the Mississippi*—from the set of twin hearts that is contained in each of the worm's six body segments—giving this night crawler a whopping total of twelve hearts! Discerning anglers prefer *D. mississippiensis* because it is a hardy little fellow that holds up well on a hook and doesn't go all floppy in the water.

What is it about the gruntin' technique that draws the worms out of the ground? The best guess is that the vibrations the agitated stob produces in the soil are similar to those made by moles and other predators digging for food. When worms feel these vibrations, they think a predator is after them, and, quite sensibly, they run for it—and end up in the buckets of the eager worm grunters.

The self-proclaimed world capital of worm gruntin' is Sopchoppy, Florida. Since 2001, the city has celebrated its favorite pastime every second Saturday in April by holding the Sopchoppy Worm Gruntin' Festival (don't forget the apostrophe, it's part of the proper spelling!). It features demonstrations, worm gruntin' competitions for kids and adults, live music, and, of course, the crowning of Worm Grunters' King and Queen. If you decide to visit the festival, don't forget to bring an appetite—there's also a worm-eating contest.

View past highlights and see what's in store for this year's festival at the official Sopchoppy worm gruntin' page, **www .wormgruntinfestival.com**.

Where Life Goes Down the Drain

WHAT: Flameless cremation

WHERE: Anderson-McQueen Funeral Home, St. Petersburg

There are countless ways to die. And cultures across time and around the globe have devised an endless array of rituals for saying good-bye to their loved ones. But for all this diversity on one hand, there have generally been just two options for the ultimate farewell: burial or burning.

Now there is a third.

In 2011, St. Petersburg's Anderson McQueen became the first funeral home in the nation to offer what it calls *flameless cremation* services to the public. Also marketed under the names *resomation* and *bio-cremation,* flameless cremation is a consumer-friendly name for the decidedly less catchy scientific term *alkaline hydrolysis* or *water resolution.* Alkaline hydrolysis is a chemical process that uses a mix of alkali and hot water to dissolve the chemical bonds in organic matter.

The funeral process employs a large stainless steel device that looks like a bank vault or an enormous front-loading washer. A hatch is opened, a corpse inserted, a button is pushed. The machine then begins to fill automatically with the correct amount of water and lye, which it heats to about 350 degrees Fahrenheit. The internal pressure also increases, to hurry along the reaction.

In plain terms, what we have here is a human-sized pressure cooker. And, yes, bio-cremation is another word for stewing—*extreme* stewing.

To Serve Mankind: Alkaline Hydrolysis

As any good cook knows, if you have a fatty, tough cut of meat—and that is, more or less, what a human body is—the best way to render it into something tender and delicate is by braising it in a gently simmering liquid.

The magic of braising lies in the structure of the protein molecules that make up a good stew meat. In its natural state, a protein is a long, coiled-up strand of amino acids. The arrangement of the amino acids and the particular bendy shape of the strand are what give each protein its unique characteristics. Damaging a protein—by, say, prolonged exposure to hot broth and acidic red wine—destroys its ability to keep its shape, causing the coil to loosen. When the protein strands uncoil, scientists say that they have become *denatured.* Regular people say they have been *cooked.*

Stewing encourages denatured protein strands to fully relax and separate, which results in fork-tender meat. (Fat and collagen play an important role in this, too, but let's keep things simple.) Now if you keep stewing away after the proteins have become denatured, the strands will eventually break down altogether. The proteins are then said to be *hydrolyzed*, which means the amino acid bonds in every strand have been completely dissolved.

This will have taken a very long time, but what once was muscle and fat and sinew is now a viscous pool of liberated amino acids oozing about in a water solution. No longer fork-tender—it's time for a spoon. Or better yet, just pour it down the drain: You wouldn't really want to eat it.

That goes double for a hydrolyzed human.

Nevertheless, what's good for the cow is good for a cadaver—with just a few non-culinary tweaks. Substitute about forty pounds of lye for the bottle of burgundy, hold the carrots and onion, and ratchet up the pressure. In just three short hours, you can hydrolyze an entire adult.

At the end of the bio-cremation process, what remains is mostly a coffee-colored sludge made up of amino acids and the few other molecules that are left over when muscle, hair, toenails, guts, brains, and other insides are dissolved down to their fundamental components. In fact, the cells have been so utterly dissolved that even the DNA is gone, so there is absolutely nothing tying the oily goo back to the person it once was. It is sterile, too, so any diseases or infections that might have plagued the deceased cannot be passed on.

When the liquid is drained off, a "shadow" skeleton remains. Consisting of pure, chalky calcium phosphate, the chemically leached bones are easily broken up into a fine powder, which can be placed in a container and returned to the next of kin.

The bio-sludge is simply poured down the drain, an unwanted by-product. However, it does make a good fertilizer.

That's flameless cremation. And if the reality behind the name makes you feel queasy, that is probably because you have never seriously looked at the alternatives of corpse disposal.

A Lose-Lose Decision

The most common funeral rite in America is burial. It strikes many as the most natural way to go—a slow decomposition back into the earth, to become forever a part of a bucolic cemetery landscape, the playground of birds and squirrels and butterflies.

But this idyllic fantasy could not be further from the truth. We process our dead very thoroughly before they enter the ground. And even then, we do our best to keep them from ever actually touching it.

First, we preserve our dearly departed by **embalming**, a process that drains them of their natural juices and pumps them full of chemical fixative—a major component of which is formaldehyde, a wicked substance that can poison you, give you cancer, *and* activate your allergies all at the same time. Next, the eternal sleepers receive a makeover to simulate that lifelike glow, they are dressed in suitably funereal attire, and, finally, they are laid out in a wooden or metal casket.

It is this 7-by-2-by-2-foot capsule of metal, wood, cloth, flesh, and chemicals that is ultimately deposited into the ground—*into* the ground but not exactly *on* it. Most cemeteries require that caskets be placed in a cement vault or at least covered with a plastic liner. These protect the casket, slow decay, and keep the turf above from sinking when the casket ultimately rots and caves in.

In the end, nature does have its way, and what once was dust to dust returns. But it takes an awful lot of junk with it. According to the Green Burial Council, a nonprofit organization that counsels for green burials, each year conventional burial puts an estimated 800,000 gallons of embalming fluid into the ground. That's in addition to the 1.6 million tons of reinforced concrete, 90,000 tons of casket steel, and the 30 million tons of hardwood that Americans dump in cemeteries every year.

Even without all the extras, a decaying corpse is still bad news. Rotting human remains that leach into the soil can poison any nearby drinking water. Viruses and many infectious bacteria survive just fine after their host has died and lurk in the ground, waiting to infect again.

Far from being a pastoral paradise, a typical cemetery is just a toxic waste dump with a nice lawn.

An increasingly popular alternative to inhumation (traditional burial) is cremation. From 1985 to 2008, the percentage of people who opted for cremation doubled; within the next decade, it is projected that more than half the people shopping for a funeral will choose burning over burial. Many who pick cremation see it as less ecologically disruptive than burial—no embalming fluid, no casket, no permanent occupation of a patch of an increasingly crowded earth. Ironically, cremation has its own set of ecological impacts that can be just as harmful.

It takes about three hours of baking at 1,600 degrees Fahrenheit to reduce an average adult to ashes, a process that releases more than 800 pounds of greenhouse gases into the atmosphere. And that is just from fueling the oven. The burning body itself generates a fine powder, called *particulate matter,* which can irritate lungs, as well as outright poisons like nitrogen oxide, carbon monoxide, hydrogen fluoride and chloride, and even mercury, if the deceased had any dental fillings.

The Shock of the New

While great strides have been made recently toward mitigating the environmental hazards of cremation and burial, a more elegant solution is not to pollute in the first place. And that is where bio-cremation re-enters our story.

Proponents of flameless cremation present it as a green choice that consumes one-third less energy and releases 75 percent less carbon dioxide than flameful cremation and that does not poison the ground like burial.

At present, Florida is the lone member of the bio-cremation vanguard, but that could change soon. Eight states already allow the practice, and more are considering it. Opponents have voiced concerns about the environmental impact of releasing large quantities of amino-acid-rich by-product into the sewage system. But by far the greatest objection to flameless cremation has been the *ick factor.* Legislators have a hard time approving any practice that critics can characterize as "pouring grandma down the drain." In New York, opponents of a 2008 proposal that would have legalized bio-cremation labeled it the "Hannibal Lecter bill." The measure was defeated.

Any ick factor associated with flameless cremation comes primarily from its unfamiliarity. After all, there is no means of treating the dead that doesn't start with a person we once knew and perhaps loved, and end with just so much bio-waste. They are all unpleasant and, to a degree, dangerous—we just don't think about that in the case of practices that have been hallowed by time and tradition.

No one can change the fact of our mortality, but innovations like flameless cremation remind us that we at least have some say in the way we make our final exit.

See also:

Embalming/tissue preservation: National Museum of Funeral History, Texas; Ward's Natural Scientific Establishment, New York

North Carolina

The Blues Lagoons

WHAT: Waste lagoons

WHERE: Eastern North Carolina

It should be clear by now that gross things can be an unsuspected source of beauty and enlightenment. When we rise to the challenge of the gross and put aside our prejudices and fears, we open ourselves to experiences that can transform our world into someplace larger and richer than we had ever imagined.

But with some gross things, however, the disgusting outer shell is as good as it gets. Scratch the surface, and all you find beneath is even more ugliness and despair.

That, unhappily, is the case with the pits of wretchedness known as *waste lagoons*.

Taking the Plunge

The 1990s were a boom time for North Carolina hog farming. In that decade, the number of North Carolina hogs went from 2.6

million to nearly 10 million, catapulting the state from the nation's eleventh-largest pork producer to second place.

Along with all the tons of bacon, pork chops, trotters, baby backs, chitterlings, and lard that was moving out of North Carolina each year, there was a huge amount of hog waste that stayed right at home. Millions of tons of feces and urine, in fact—more than is produced annually by the human population of Los Angeles, Chicago, and New York *combined*.

Farm waste doesn't go down the drain to be processed with everyone else's poop down at the municipal sewer. Farm waste is the farmer's problem. Now, a little manure is a good thing. Ever since the first agriculturist put a leash on a goat and tilled his wheat field by hand, the engine that drives the farm economy has been the cycle of farmers feeding produce to their animals and fertilizing their crops with animal waste.

But the massive scale of North Carolina's hog farms has overwhelmed the ability of the local environment to process the waste. The animal leavings have to be collected into huge open-air pits, euphemistically called *lagoons*. But nothing could be further from the image of a white-sand tropical atoll with limpid, teal-colored waters. A waste lagoon at a modern CAFO (that's *concentrated animal feeding operation*, the industrialized version of what we used to call *a farm*) is a 12-foot-deep pit up to 10 acres in expanse that holds tens of millions of gallons of—there are no other words for it—*pig piss and crap.*

The smell is appalling. It gets into clothes and never washes out. On bad days, it can trap neighbors in their homes for miles around. Winds whipping over the lagoon can aerosolize the waste, blowing up a fecal haze that irritates lungs and eyes. Yes, in rural North Carolina, they have sewage smog.

They also have a thing called *fishkills*. These are caused when heavy rains and other bad weather cause the lagoons to spill. The runoff can reach lakes, rivers, or estuaries. The sudden influx of fertilizer causes algae to go wild and overproduce in vast colonies called *algae blooms*. This plant activity pulls the oxygen out of the nearby water, and, consequently, all the fish start to suffocate. That is a fishkill. In one event in 2005, a single river lost a billion fish.

That's not even the whole grievous tale of waste lagoons, but it's enough. Even the most hardened aficionado of the gross needs to know when to call it quits.

While the problem of pig waste is very difficult to manage, it is not intractable. In 2007, North Carolina became the first state to ban new construction and expansion of waste lagoons for hogs. It also began a pilot program to encourage farms to capture methane from the lagoons and **convert it into electricity**.

See also:

"Convert it into electricity": Park Spark poop-fueled light, Massachusetts

THE NORTHEAST

Washington, D.C.

The Soapman Cometh

WHAT: The Soapman

WHERE: The National Museum of Natural
History, the Smithsonian Institution

Browsing the 136 million items spread throughout the galleries of the Smithsonian's nineteen museums is like rummaging through the nation's attic: Here is a tennis racket with broken strings (used by champion Chris Evert); over there, an obsolete Game Boy (the 1989 debut model). What's with that ratty brier pipe with a hole chewed through the stem? (Einstein's.) Anyone want a plastic and titanium artificial heart or a screaming yellow Pac-Man gumball bank? And what can that be over there, billowing ostentatiously from that mannequin? Barbara Eden's harem pants from *I Dream of Genie*? Nope, a tragic pair of **Zouave pantaloons** worn by someone's great-great-great-grandfather in the War Between the States, because he thought they made him look cool.

What you see in the cases is only the tip of the iceberg. Many of the items in the complete collection are too trivial, too fragile, or too disturbing for public viewing, so they are stored in a network of vaults, chambers, shelves, and refrigerators that the general public never get to see.

One such item is the *Soapman*. It looks like a recumbent, life-size figure, crudely rendered out of raw-umber- and sienna-colored clay and fitted with a pair of incongruous silk knee socks. The medium, however, is not clay, but a waxy substance known as *adipocere*, and the Soapman is not a sculpture.

It's a real human being.

You're Not Being Soft-Soaped

Reaching us through the delicate indirection of the French language, *adipocere* literally means *fat-wax*. Some people prefer to use the straightforwardly English expressions *grave wax* or *corpse wax*. But by whichever name you choose to call it, there is a case of mistaken identity at work, for the phenomenon in question is not wax at all: It is really human *soap*.

Soap is nothing more than a special form of fat. (It's the salt of a fatty acid, for those of you keeping score.) In principle, soap making is quite simple. Just take fat trimmings from your leftovers, mix them with lye (in a ratio of about 1 part lye to 5 parts fat, by weight), and boil in water. Skim off the fatty goo that bubbles to the surface, and when it cools, you will have soap—a very nasty smelling, harsh soap, but soap nonetheless.

From the harshest farm-caldron lye soap to the silkiest, cucumber-scented spa moisturizing bar, all soaps derive their cleansing property from the same peculiar molecular structure. One end of a soap molecule is *hydrophilic*, that is, it bonds readily to water; the other end is *hydrophobic*, or repelled by water. When you lather up in the shower, the hydrophobic molecule tips bond with the oils on your skin. This greasy emulsion is then rinsed down the drain when water from the tap grabs on to the soap by its hydrophilic end.

The technical word for soap making is *saponification* (from *sapo* the Latin for *soap*). Chemically speaking, saponification—as some of you might have perceived—is just another term for **alkali hydrolysis**.

Given the right circumstances—an airless, cold, wet, and alkaline environment plus the right microbial mix—saponification can occur spontaneously, causing the fat cells in a decomposing body to turn into so-called corpse wax. As the deteriorating muscles wither, the newly formed adipocere oozes into nooks and crannies, where it solidifies. This led the first observers who documented soap corpses to mistakenly believe that the entire body had undergone a transformation. Actually, the process is more like colonization, where the grave wax migrates into spaces that other tissue is retreating from. This invasion continues until the supply of corpse wax runs out. Accordingly, adipocere occurs most in obese individuals, who have more fuel, so to speak, to keep the chemical reaction going.

Grave wax is immune to microbial decomposition, so a body that has undergone relatively advanced saponification can stay preserved for hundreds of years. Because the hardened adipocere is quite brittle and flaky, the greatest danger to the soap-corpse is actually breakage. That is the reason why the Soapman was removed from display in 1991 and moved to the museum's protected Dry Environment room.

In the early stages of saponification, the liquescent body

reportedly smells strongly of ammonia or rancid cheese. But as the process completes and the corpse wax hardens, the smell dissipates.

A Scientific Soap Opera

The Soapman first appeared in 1875, in the possession of a Dr. Joseph Leidy of Philadelphia and—remarkably enough—in the company of a Soap Lady.

Distinguished professor of anatomy at the University of Philadelphia and president of the city's Academy of Natural Sciences, Dr. Leidy was a formidable figure in intellectual circles. Born in 1823, Leidy began his career in the era of the **dilettante gentleman naturalist** and ended it in the age of specialist scientist. A member of a dying breed of polymaths, Leidy was dubbed by recent biographer Leonard Warren *"the last man who knew everything."*

That is almost not an exaggeration. Dr. Leidy studied dinosaur fossils and other New World novelties and was one of the founders of American vertebrate paleontology. He named hundreds of species of plant, animal, and fungus. He identified the nematode in raw pork that causes trichinosis. Leidy was also the world's first CSI agent: In 1846, he became the first person to use microscopic analysis of bloodstains to identify a murderer.

Dr. Leidy may have solved one forensic riddle, but he created an even knottier one with his mysterious adipocere couple, which he split up and donated to two Philadelphia medical museums. The woman went to the **Mütter Museum**, the man to the University of Philadelphia (which eventually ceded him to the Smithsonian).

Dr. Leidy himself left no definitive account of how the soap couple came into his possession. However, through the paperwork he filed and recollections of individuals who discussed the remarkable bequests with him, a bare-bones narrative of the soap couple emerged. Their mortal name was *Ellenbogen* or *von Ellenbogen*, and they died of yellow fever in 1792. Both were in their sixties. The couple had been unearthed in Philadelphia, from a cemetery at Fourth and Race Streets that was being moved on account of some undefined urban renovation project. It was the caretaker, who knew Leidy by reputation, who had alerted him to the medically intriguing specimens.

In 1942 Dr. James McFarland, then curator of the Mütter Museum, attempted to verify the story. He discovered that every element of it was false: The yellow fever outbreak was in 1793, not 1792, there were no Ellenbogens in Philadelphia before 1836, and there was no cemetery at Fourth and Race, ever.

X-ray analysis of the Soap Lady in 1987 determined that she died at about the age of 40. It also discovered in the tattered remains of her clothing pins and buttons that were not manufactured until the 1820s, which put her time of death sometime after that. A 1994 analysis of the Soapman corroborated the dating. It established that he was also in his 40s.

Chances are that the esteemed Dr. Leidy was not an inveterate liar, but that he was trying to cover his tracks and protect his sources. Preeminent scientist and respected member of the community though he might be, Leidy was still technically guilty of **grave robbing**—a crime that in Philadelphia, with its burgeoning population of student doctors, was neither completely unknown nor unpunished.

The National Museum of Natural History is open every day,

except Christmas. Admission is free. For more information, go to **www.mnh.si.edu**.

See also:

Dilettante gentleman naturalist: Ward's Natural Science Establishment, New York

Grave robbing: Cemetery gun, Pennsylvania

Mütter Museum, Pennsylvania

Zouave pantaloons: National Museum of Funeral History, Houston

Maryland

This Might Be Hard to Swallow

WHAT: Human hairball

WHERE: National Museum of Health
and Medicine, Silver Spring

This world-class medical museum and treasure trove of morbidity is so extensive that there is almost nothing you can say about it. For once you start to list even a selection of collection highlights, you can find yourself embarked on a descriptive path that stretches far beyond the horizon.

Founded as the Army Medical Museum in 1862, one year into the Civil War, the institution was created expressly as a repository for medically intriguing specimens culled from the battlefields of the nation's bloodiest and most brutal war—which, one supposes, is one way to make lemonade from life's lemons.

William Hammond, US Army Surgeon General at this tumultuous time, directed his medical officers to collect "all specimens of morbid anatomy, surgical or medical, which may be regarded as valuable; together with projectiles and foreign bodies removed; and such other matter as may prove of interest in the study of military medicine and surgery."

And that is exactly what they did. In the three remaining years of fighting, army surgeons harvested 5,000 skeletal remains and 10,000 preserved organs. Big, round numbers easily lose their meaning, but, once you recall that each of these specimens was once a living person who had other priorities than to end up providing an object-lesson in battlefield surgery, both the horror and the audacity of this enterprise become immediately clear.

On its very grand scale, however, the Army Medical Museum was merely replicating a project that other medical institutions across the globe had already been doing for a generation. Surgeon General Hammond was aiming to assemble a national **pathology cabinet**, the largest and most comprehensive reference to human injury and disease anywhere in the world.

The data the battlefield doctors collected was analyzed and eventually compiled as *The Medical and Surgical History of the War of Rebellion, 1861–1865*. Published in six volumes between 1870 and 1883, the collection was a seminal work of American pathology.

Although the Army Medical Museum was founded as a working research institution, by the end of the nineteenth century the museum, with its racks of spectacularly damaged specimens, was already a popular attraction for ordinary citizens, who went there to savor the same delightfully naughty *frisson* of openly gawking at the human body, in all its glorious gore, that still draws spectators there today.

A Plethora of Pathology

The surrender at Appomattox ended the Civil War, but army surgeons continued their diligent collecting. From frontier skirmishes, they sent back samples of human detritus from cavalrymen and Indian braves alike. George Otis, curator from 1864–1881, whose great passion was **skull collecting**, widened the scope and used the resources of the museum to net almost a thousand crania from all six inhabited continents.

Today, the museum's collection comprises 25 million items. With room to show only a tiny fraction of its archive, the museum displays are changed as frequently as the menu at a trendy locavore bistro. But a few perennial favorites remain on permanent view—items such as the bullet that killed Abraham Lincoln and the severed leg of General Dan Sickles, mounted alongside the cannonball that blew it off. Another crowd-pleaser is the developmental anatomy exhibit, with its case of fetal skeletons arrayed like a diminutive kick line of Radio City Rockettes.

With so much gross to choose from, it might surprise you that one of the museum's most sought-out displays is a hairball. But it's a doozy.

The scientific name for *hairball* is *trichobezoar*. *Trichos* is a form of *thrix*, the Greek word for *hair*. And *bezoar* (pronounced *BEE-zohr*) comes from Persian—*bet you didn't see that coming!*—and it means something like *antidote*.

Bezoar is a general term for any clump of indigestible material that forms in the stomach. The word was introduced to Europe in the eleventh century, when Middle-Eastern merchants began selling these petrified lumps as magical talismans that offered protection against poisoning. They remained a popular remedy until the eighteenth century.

There are four types of bezoar, and each takes its name from the stuff it is made from: milk solids (*lactobezoar*), plant fiber (*phytobezoar*), unmetabolized medicine (*pharmacobezoar*), or hair. (Persimmons are particularly great producers of bezoars, so much so that, even though they are plants, they get to have their own name as a subclass, which is *diospyrobezoar*.)

The most familiar trichobezoars are the ones domesticated cats leave on your living room carpet, but cattle are also prone to them. Worse for the poor cows, their six chambers of stomachs present a maze from which it is very difficult to regurgitate a growing hairball, so most bovine bezoars stay inside.

The museum owns twenty-seven hairballs, but most stay in storage and make only rare public appearances. Twenty-four come from animals (the unlikeliest being a chicken, who got hers from compulsively grooming her dog companion). That means three came from people—including the museum's star attraction: a trichobezoar surgically removed from a twelve-year-old girl who suffered from *trichophagia*, or compulsive hair nibbling, and which had grown inside her for six years. The horn-shaped obstruction of matted, golden-brown hair is almost four handspans in length and is still molded into the shape of the girl's stomach.

Trichobezoars are not necessarily painful, although they can cause cramps and bloating, and they are dangerous because wiry hair tips can puncture the stomach wall.

If you want to check out the mighty trichobezoar or enjoy other examples of morbid anatomy, you can visit the museum any day of the year but Christmas. It's free, too, but you might want to leave a donation to express your appreciation. Find out more at **www.medicalmuseum.mil**.

See also:
Pathology cabinet: Syphilitic brains, Indiana
Skull collecting: The Morton Skull Collection, Pennsylvania

Ring of Fire

WHAT: Antique anti-spermatorrhea device

WHERE: The William P. Didusch Center
for Urologic History, Linthicum

Housed in the American Urological Association headquarters, the Center for Urologic History is named after its founder and first curator, William P. Didusch, who is somewhat more widely recognized as having been American's foremost urological illustrator. The museum displays Didusch's work and other historic medical illustrations, along with hundreds of urological tools of the trade, including cytoscopes, resectoscopes, laparoscopes, lithotriptors, and catheters—a host of diabolical instruments that doctors have used over the ages to sneak a peek up the urethra and remove the impediments that nature alone no longer can.

It's a three-hundred-year sweep of history that leads from the early and extremely dangerous kidney-stone surgeries to modern ultrasound treatment that pulverizes these jagged mineral clumps without any need to enter the body, and the Center for Urologic History covers it all—including the medical dead ends that leave us moderns both scratching our heads in puzzlement and cowering with vicarious terror.

One particularly vicious, and thankfully obsolete, device you can see is the outlandishly named *spermatorrhea ring*. Its purpose was to prevent nocturnal ejaculation, and as recently as 1903 you could purchase one from the Sears Roebuck catalogue for a quarter. This implement of moral rectitude is a double ring of metal. The inner ring clips over the penis, while the outer ring, which is lined on the inside with an armature of blunt metal teeth, constitutes what could be called the *medically active ingredient*. In the event of nocturnal erection, the sensitive skin of the engorged part expands against the spiky outer ring, and the sleeper is pricked into consciousness in time to prevent nature from committing an unspeakable crime against itself.

Getting a Grip on the Solitary Vice

The Victorians who dreamed up devices like the spermatorrhea ring were infamously squeamish about sexual matters, and in the case of masturbation they were practically hysterical. But that's not the way things always had been. The ancients were relatively tolerant of sexual matters. In classical Greece and Rome, more or less anything went, as long as the amorous peccadilloes of a man—and it was almost always men they were talking about—didn't interfere with his work, and as long as he pursued them in a sufficiently macho way. (Romans, to some extent, and ancient Athenians, in particular, didn't object to men having sex with other men in principle; they just didn't like them to be girly about it.)

It is a cliché to blame the end of sexual freedom in the Western world on the rise of Christianity. But it's a cliché that happens to be largely true. Under the influence of St. Augustine of Hippo (who was writing around 400 CE) and the much more severe St. Thomas Aquinas, who lived eight hundred years later, the church promoted chastity as the ideal, with sex within marriage coming in as a second-place compromise. Anything else was a nonstarter.

The particular obsession with masturbation, however, did not really begin until the seventeenth century. One of the first texts to single-mindedly demonize the practice was a pamphlet that took its name from Onan, that biblical figure who, enduring a humiliation even worse than Job's, will forever be identified with self-abuse. *Onania; or the Heinous Sin of Self-Pollution and All its Frightful Consequences in Both Sexes Consider'd; With Spiritual and Physical Advice to Those Who Have Already Injured Themselves by this Abominable Practice* first appeared in London sometime around 1710. It became a publishing sensation. By midcentury it had gone through more than twenty editions, in both England and the American colonies. Each edition was expanded to include reader-submitted testimonials to the demoralizing effects of the solitary vice. Ultimately the landmark work grew to more than three times its original size, swelling to over three hundred lurid pages.

As its subtitle implies, *Onania* was primarily a moral broadside. It attacked masturbation as a selfish and antisocial vice that arrogantly flouts the divine mandate to be fruitful and multiply. It took a physician, however, the Swiss-born Samuel-August-André-David Tissot, to bolster the moral case with the weight of medical science. Published in 1758, Tissot's *L'Onanisme*, subtitled "a dissertation on the illnesses caused by masturbation," is the seminal medical text on the dangers of excessive semen loss.

Practicing his trade in the era of **humoral medicine**, Tissot believed that sickness arose from an imbalance of essential bodily fluids. He called semen "the Essential Oil of the animal liquors" and elevated its importance above that of the four more familiar humors described by the Roman physician Galen: blood, phlegm, yellow bile, and black bile. Tissot argued that depleting the body of semen debilitated all the other humors, weakening the body generally even as it caused a gantlet of specific medical disorders, including impotence, blindness, deafness, madness, and tuberculosis. Loss of but a single ounce of semen, in Tissot's estimation, was worse than losing 40 ounces of blood. (To put this in perspective, losing 70 ounces of blood would kill most of us outright.)

Given the role of semen in reproduction, it makes intuitive sense that this fluid might somehow embody a sort of vital force that fulfills a more general life-sustaining function in the body. It's an intuition that happens to be completely wrong.

Soon after the turn of the nineteenth century, physicians rejected Galen and the theory of humors. But the stigma against masturbation was so strong that they continued to accept Tissot's dire medical claims, even though these made sense only within Galen's now-debunked system.

The weakness in the medical case against masturbation was papered over by adopting a new and impressively scientific-sounding diagnosis. *Spermatorrhea* (from the Greek *spermata* + *rheën*, meaning *to gush forth seeds*) became the preferred term in medical circles. In its widest definition, spermatorrhea covered the excessive loss of semen by any means other than married intercourse (and sometimes, even *that* was included). Under this deceptively simple umbrella term, matters of physiology, pathology, and morality were conflated into a single, thoroughly confusing muddle. Sex with a professional, loving but unmarried sex, cheating on a spouse, regular old masturbation, and genuine physiological conditions like nocturnal emissions or just a chronic low-level drip, the spermatological equivalent of incontinence, were all considered aspects of the same overarching disease. *Spermatorrhea* might have sounded more scientific, but it was ultimately an unstable and unworkable concept. And still lurking behind it was a conceptual holdover from the exploded system of Galenic medicine—that losing sperm was akin to losing one's vital essence.

Yankees Say "*No!*" to Yanking

On the Puritanical shores of America, the seed of anti-masturbation fervor fell on fertile soil. Tissot's ideas reached our nation in the 1830s, just as the religious revival movement known as the *Second Great Awakening* was gaining steam. It was a time of amazing energy and innovation in popular religion. New sects were proliferating under charismatic leaders, who often espoused radically egalitarian ideas about the races and the sexes. So, on the progressive end of the balance, both the abolitionist and the women's suffrage movements emerge from this period— but, on the other side, under the evangelical zeal of the Great Awakening, nearly every aspect of sexuality was heavily stigmatized. In some of the newly emerging sects, even sex between married partners was considered unhealthy, a necessary evil to be indulged only enough to perpetuate the species. One group, the United Society of Believers in Christ's Second Appearing, derisively known as *the Shakers* because of their dithyrambic style of worship, were forbidden sex altogether. It was only by conversion, not reproduction, that the denomination kept from dying off.

The Shakers are an extreme case, but even the most mainstream denominations at that time could agree that sex for fun was indisputably a sin. Even from a secular point of view, the best that could be said about recreational sex was that it was a wasteful activity that robbed a healthy person of vigor that could be turned to more profitable ends than animal pleasure.

Founding Father and influential physician **Benjamin Rush** was the first American doctor to embrace Tissot's polemic against masturbation. One of Rush's fields of expertise was mental illness, and he was particularly receptive to Tissot's argument that semen depletion was a cause of madness. That idea may seem insane today, but at least Rush and Tissot were operating within the medical mainstream as it existed in their day. Many of Tissot's later popularizers were nothing less than crackpots by any standard.

Presbyterian minister and outspoken sex-shamer Sylvester Graham held that excitement of *any* kind exercised a baleful influence over body and soul. Fiery foods attracted his ire no less than saucy sex. Consequently, Graham advocated a spice-free, vegetarian diet, which he thought would dampen sexual urges, and, thus, free one from the specter of dissipation, insanity, and blindness. Graham gained some celebrity as a public lecturer on the tragedy of self-abuse. To enraptured audiences, he would explain how to recognize the chronic masturbator by his sallow, pimply complexion and furtive manner. And to those in thrall of the secret vice, Graham promised an agonizing death as their bodies rebelled against the insuperable insult that had been inflicted upon it. Today this quixotic thinker is remembered for inventing the graham cracker, which he designed to be the perfect antiaphrodisiac.

Next in line in the vanguard of anti-masturbation activists was Dr. John Harvey Kellogg, inventor of the Kellogg corn flake, which was marketed by his brother and future breakfast cereal baron, Will Keith Kellogg. Dr. Kellogg ran a highly successful health spa in Battle Creek, Michigan, where he put into practice some of the hygienic ideas pioneered by Sylvester Graham. An early proponent of what we would call *holistic health,* Kellogg regarded physical, psychological, and moral health as an indivisible whole that could be improved through a strict regimen of diet, exercise, and self-discipline. High among his priorities was sexual abstinance; only slightly lower on the list were frequent enemas.

Kellogg viewed masturbation as "the most dangerous of all sexual abuses, because the most extensively practiced," and he took a very forceful approach to its suppression. For starters, he recommended that children be inoculated against this deadly vice by being confronted at an early age with vivid depictions of the diabolical torments that awaited the sexually incontinent in the next world as well as medical afflictions they could expect in this one. For Kellogg, the list of infirmities included nervous exhaustion, tuberculosis, indigestion, heart disease, sore throat, epilepsy, poor vision and hearing, partial or complete paralysis, and insanity. If this gentle persuasion of reason failed, Kellogg recommended more direct action: Hands could be tied to the bed frame at night, or the genitalia could be securely wrapped. In the most incorrigible of cases, circumcision, without anesthetic, was demanded, "as the brief pain attending the operation will have a salutary effect upon the mind."

In light of Dr. Kellogg's muscular prescriptions, the spermatorrhea ring might almost seem a humane alternative. It was only one of many quack inventions that abounded from the mid-nineteenth to early twentieth centuries. Trusses, metal sheaths, restraints of all sorts, and even electrical devices were all sold to fearful parents, anxious to spare their children from the deathly heartbreak of self-love.

The William P. Didusch Center for Urologic History is open to

the public, but only by appointment. Even if you have no intention of visiting in person, you should check out their website,
which features a searchable collections archive, virtual exhibits,
and lovely brochures on plagues, quack medicine, the history of
sex, and more topics of grossological interest, which can be
downloaded for free: **urologichistory.museum**.

See also:

Benjamin Rush, **Humoral medicine:** Lewis and Clark's latrines,
    Montana

Pennsylvania

Death at the Cemetery

WHAT: Cemetery gun

WHERE: Museum of Mourning Art,
Arlington Cemetery, Drexel Hill

Located in an operating cemetery, the Museum of Mourning Art presents itself not just as an educational institution, but as an actual work of mourning intended to comfort the bereaved. The museum is housed in a replica of George Washington's Mount Vernon estate, which definitely sets a tone. But if you can get past the Daughters of the American Revolution fastidiousness, you will be rewarded with a nice selection of antique funerary *objets d'art*.

The selection is strictly Anglo-American, but what the collection lacks in scope it compensates for in depth. There are some wonderful Victorian mourning clothes, a beautifully preserved horse-drawn hearse, and one of the nation's best assemblages of mourning jewelry in one place.

There is also one incongruous object that strikes a refreshingly discordant note amid the WASP-y solemnity. It is a chunky, wooden and iron device, scarred by use and darkened with age, mounted by a pivot onto an even more abused wooden block. The main body of this decrepit item is outfitted with a wheel-lock mechanism, whose exposed parts are dull with a thick patina of age. A short length of rusty chain hangs from one end, and a stubby muzzle juts from the front.

The purpose of this extremely rare artifact is not to mourn the dead but to smite the living. It's called a *cemetery gun*, and this antique weapon was used to guard against a similarly antique crime: *grave robbing*.

A Visit from the Resurrectionist

No, it is not some sacrilege imagined in Edgar Allan Poe stories or Boris Karloff movies. Grave robbing at one time was an actual, for-real crime. From the middle of the eighteenth century until almost the end of the nineteenth, the threat of body snatching in major metropolitan areas loomed so large that it caused serious anxiety and even civic unrest, particularly among the poor, who were its most frequent victims.

Unlike many crime waves, which arise from an array of personal and historical forces that can be difficult to identify and untangle, the rise and fall of grave robbing can be traced back to one simple factor: the demand for cadavers in medical schools.

The first legal provision for medical cadavers in the English-speaking world dates from the reign of Henry VIII. By royal edict, the bodies of a certain number of executed criminals each year were to be made available to medical schools. The decision was made as much in the interest of rough-and-tumble "justice" as medicine—the "desecration" of dissection being regarded as the Crown's final legal nose-thumbing to the very worst malefactors.

In an age when medicine was treated more like a branch of philosophy than an applied science, medical schools were content to dissect just one or two cadavers each year while the entire student body watched, and the arrangement worked. But in the very empirical eighteenth century, a sound, practical understanding of anatomy was increasingly seen as essential to medical practice—after all, as pioneering surgeons like London's *William Hunter* most reasonably asked, how can a doctor hope to fix a sick body if he doesn't know what a healthy one looks like? Hunter began to lure pupils to his private surgical school by offering each student a body of his own to dissect. (Procurement of those cadavers was left to the wiles of his soon-to-be equally famous brother, **John Hunter**.) The one-to-one dissection ratio was so popular with students that medical schools throughout Britain were forced to follow suit. Soon the practice spread to America.

Now, in the 1700s, a person could be executed for some pretty trivial offenses, but criminal enterprise and the hangman's noose simply could not keep pace with the new demand for medical corpses. A chronic shortage of cadavers became a perverse incentive for medical schools to skirt the law in their search for steady supplies.

John Hunter and the other men tasked with supplying anatomy departments started to form relationships with a new class of criminal entrepreneurs, known as *resurrectionists* or *body-snatchers,* who, for a price, would provide cadavers, no questions asked.

In its classic form, grave robbing entailed sneaking into graveyards under cover of darkness and exhuming recently interred corpses. The most active times of year were fall and winter, when the students were at their studies, the nights were long and dark, and the cold kept the corpses from stinking too much. Wooden shovels were the preferred tool, because they made less noise than metal.

A more subtle way of obtaining cadavers was to have an agent, usually a woman, visit a prison hospital or a home for the indigent. Pretending to be a relative of some newly deceased inmate, she would claim the body "for burial." A little bribery often facilitated the process.

The association with grave robbing was a terrible stain on the medical profession, ironically, at a time when it was beginning to make significant practical advances and when the general quality of physicians was improving.

Body snatching peaked in Britain in late 1827 when a pair of rogues named Burke and Hare realized that stealing corpses was harder work than simply manufacturing them. Burke and Hare were responsible for anywhere between sixteen and thirty murders. At a going rate of up to £10 a head (the equivalent of about $1,000 today), the rewards were worth the risk. The pair's murderous spree terrorized the citizens of Edinburgh for a year, and helped usher in Britain's 1832 Anatomy Act, which granted medical schools access to unclaimed bodies from hospitals and poorhouses. Similar laws were enacted in the US, but they varied greatly from state to state and were sometimes repealed or ignored because dissection was a controversial practice still widely viewed as corpse desecration. It wasn't until 1880 that most medical schools in the United States had access to an ample and secure supply of cadavers.

Although it was championed early on by the intellectual elite, who not infrequently offered their own bodies to be autopsied after death, dissection was wildly unpopular among the lower classes—who, unwillingly, unasked, and unrecompensed, were the ones who actually supplied most of the cadavers that made their way to anatomy classrooms.

As the terror of the body-snatching phenomenon grew in American cities, predictable patterns of panic set in. There was occasional mob violence, as allegations of grave robbing ignited riots and near lynchings. There were also free-market responses. People who could afford it buried loved ones in guarded graveyards or under heavy stone vaults. A number of anti-body-snatching devices went up for sale, too. One, called a *mortsafe*, was an iron cage that fitted over the grave, thus preventing exhumation.

Another was the cemetery gun. This automated weapon, mounted on a free-spinning shaft, would be planted near a grave and was activated by means of a trip wire. When the wire was pulled, the gun would pivot and discharge, roughly in the direction of the disturbance. That the gun did not aim was a less pernicious design flaw than the fact that it did not disarm itself in the morning, either.

This ill-conceived public menace was not particularly successful, and it was eventually outlawed.

You can view the cemetery gun along with more conventional funerary artifacts at the Museum of Mourning Art at Arlington Cemetery, just outside Philadelphia. Admission is by appointment only, so call (610) 259-5800 in advance.

A premonitory word to the wise: This museum may be dedicated entirely to death and mourning, but it decidedly does *not* revel in morbidity. If you're a person who does—and we suspect you *do*—you might want to keep that on the down-low during your visit, or be prepared for a dose of disapproval.

See also:
John Hunter: McDowell House, Kentucky
Mourning art: Leila's Hair Museum, Missouri

From the Bowels of the Medical Archives

WHAT: The Mega Colon

WHERE: The Mütter Museum at the College
of Physicians of Philadelphia

This Philadelphia shrine to morbid anatomy is the undisputed monarch of North American medical museums.

Although the 25 million specimens of the National Museum of Health may dwarf the holdings of the museum of the College of Physicians of Philadelphia, every item at this exquisite jewel of morbidity is pure gold, without a single grain of dross.

The Mütter boasts its own 139-piece **skull collection**, its own **soap person**, and jars of **syphilitic brains**. It also has a two-headed one-bodied baby, a two-bodied one-headed baby, and other preserved specimens of *teratology*, or abnormal development; a plaster cast of the conjoined brothers Chang and Eng, who gave the world the term *Siamese twins*; and the cancer-ridden hard palate of President Grover Cleveland, which was removed in a secret operation aboard a private yacht, because in 1893 cancer was so misunderstood and dreaded a disease that not even its name could be uttered in polite society.

Where the former Army Medical Museum offers the bullet that slew President Lincoln and fragments of the Great Emancipator's skull, the Mütter has laid claim to the *entire* brain of his assassin, celebrated actor and Confederate revanchist John

Wilkes Booth, *plus* the brain of lesser-known presidential assassin Charles Guiteau, whose revolver cut short the administration of James Garfield.

Best of all, every one of these items is right out on public display, not cloistered away for the credentialed few.

The Guru of Gross

It is impossible to overstate the role the Mütter Museum has played in introducing the joy of morbid anatomy to a broader public and to raising the general esteem of all things gross in our nation. And most of that credit belongs to its longtime curator, Gretchen Worden, who helmed the museum from 1982 until her death in 2004.

When Worden joined the museum in the 1970s, it was an institution in deep decline, known only to a handful of antiquarians, weirdos, and medical historians. But in 1858, when Thomas Dent Mütter donated his personal collection of morbid anatomy to the College of Physicians of Philadelphia, it was quite a different story.

The institution, founded in 1787, was not a teaching college but an association of *colleagues*, professional physicians who pooled their knowledge and resources to expand the frontiers of medicine. The infusion of Mütter's hundreds of pathological models, bones, and preserved organs—not to mention the $30,000 in cash he left for the collection's maintenance—propelled the college's formerly modest but respectable pathological collection squarely into national prominence.

In its quest to grow into a comprehensive archive of physical disease and dysfunction, the expanding museum acquired many items that might seem to us more at home in a circus sideshow—

like the wax model of a woman with a 9-inch horn growing out of her forehead, or the photographs of the legless girl who learned to walk with her hands, or the Chevalier Jackson collection of thousands of utterly random swallowed items—including safety pins, matchsticks, good luck charms, keys, and crucifixes—which the prolific Dr. Jackson removed from the throats, lungs, and stomachs of his patients.

Changes within the medical profession made pathology collections less relevant by the end of the nineteenth century, and the rise of photography, which allowed high-quality images to be captured in mass-produced books, was the final nail in the coffin. There was no longer any need for real-life reference collections like the Mütter. As their original medical purpose receded into history, these pathological cabinets were increasingly regarded as simply ghoulish and bizarre oddities from the distant past.

When Gretchen Worden began her tenure as curator of the Mütter, she adopted a counterintuitive policy. Rather than try to suppress the museum's creepy legacy, she embraced it. Worden savored the eerie power of the collection to simultaneously fascinate and repel, and believed that she could attract an audience that felt the same way. But she also never lost sight of the fact that every specimen had its own story to tell—not only about the body, how it works, and how it goes awry, but also the individual story of the person it once was. Every specimen was human and deserved respect.

The course Worden charted garnered tremendous support and even affection from a wide variety of constituencies—from goths and steampunks at the countercultural fringes to parents with small children, educators, artists, scientists, and patrons with blue blood and deep pockets. The unlikely coalition has endured almost thirty years.

And the Winner Is ...

So far we have managed to remain relatively dignified while stoking the appetite for gross-outs. But in this one case, let's drop any pretense of redeeming social importance. Let us twist the dial all the way to eleven and reach for the pinnacle of grotesquerie and bad taste: Our featured item at the Mütter Museum and nominee for the nation's grossest artifact is the Mega Colon.

With its twisty, knobby shape and its papery, yellow-brown skin, this 8-foot-long monstrosity, which measures 27 inches around at its widest girth, looks like an immense fingerling potato, although it is closer kin to a blood sausage. This prodigious pathological specimen is more than twice as long as a healthy colon and about three times as fat.

The unlucky owner of this morbidly distended colon was a sideshow performer, who, taking what meager advantage he could of his affliction, billed himself as the *Balloon Man* and the *Human Windbag*.

The Balloon Man suffered from Hirschsprung's disease, a disorder in which the nerves in sections of the colon (the last stretch of large intestine before the rectum and freedom) fail to develop. Unable to receive the necessary signals, the colon cannot contract and ease its contents along their way. The result is terrible, chronic constipation. Hirschsprung's did the poor Balloon Man in before he turned 30.

When the organ was removed during autopsy, the Balloon Man's colon contained 40 pounds of feces. (Don't pretend you didn't want to know.)

The Mütter Museum is open every day except Thanksgiving, Christmas Eve, Christmas Day, and New Year's. General admission is the best $15 you've ever spent, with student and senior discounts. Kids are free. Go to **www.collphyphil.org** for more information.

See also:

Skull collection: Morton skull collection, Pennsylvania

Soap person: The Smithsonian, National Museum of Natural History, Washington, D.C.

Syphilitic brains: Indiana Museum of Medical History, Indiana

A *Head* of His Time

WHAT: Morton Skull Collection

WHERE: Museum of Archaeology and Anthropology, University of Pennsylvania, Philadelphia

Sometime in 1830, an anatomy professor at Pennsylvania Medi-

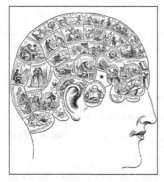

A phrenology chart

cal College was preparing a lecture on the hot new theory of the *Five Races of Man.* Exasperated that he could only get his hands on cranial specimens of *four* of the said races, he decided to start his own skull collection so that he would never be similarly embarrassed again.

The professor in question, Samuel George Morton, a well-connected, well-liked pillar of his community, mobilized a global network of friends, colleagues, and business associates whom he flattered, wheedled, and bribed into supporting his cause. In just one year, they netted him one hundred human skulls, plucked from battlefields, purloined from graves, and purchased with few questions from shady adventurers who'd done and seen God-only-knows-what in distant corners of the globe.

By the time Morton died in 1851, his cranial collection had grown to 867 items—its sheer prodigiousness earned it the nickname the *American Golgotha*—and the man himself had written the book on heads, quite literally. In fact, he had done it twice.

But the dark legacy of Morton's craniological research condemned this gentle and somewhat frail academic to be remembered in history as the architect of the intellectual cesspool known as *scientific racism*.

What Is the True Measure of Man?

The five races that Morton was attempting to illustrate when he was struck by the idea for his skull collection were part of a *taxonomic*, or naming, system conceived by a German naturalist named *Johann Friedrich Blumenbach* at the very end of the eighteenth century. The branches in our collective family tree that he identified were the *Caucasian, Mongolian, Malayan, Ethiopian,* and *American*, but they might be more familiar as the *white, yellow, brown, black,* and *red* races.

Blumenbach defined the races, but he did not explicitly rank them. That, however, was the implicit next step, and Samuel Morton was the one to take it.

When we speak of race today, we usually reference skin color or place of origin. But the methodology pioneered by Blumenbach placed especial significance on the features of the face and head. Working within this scheme, Morton applied himself to refining Blumenbach's guidelines based on precise observation. Whenever Morton received a new skull, he identified it according to racial type, and then he proceeded to make a series of pains-taking craniometric measurements, including the cubic capacity of each cranium as well as the angle of forehead slope.

All these facial measurements were really just an indirect means of approaching the brain. By the eighteenth century, it was an accepted fact, at least among the scientific community, that the brain was the organ of consciousness, but how it functioned was an utter mystery. The conclusions Morton drew about the hierarchy of races followed from connections that were assumed to exist between the shape of a skull and the quality of the brain housed within it. After examining hundreds of skulls, Morton pronounced that those of Caucasians possess on average the largest volume and straightest brows, and concluded that therefore the white race must be the most intellectually gifted.

He went further still. Most naturalists of the day, Blumenbach included, subscribed to the idea that there was but one species of *Homo sapiens*, which had diversified into the several races, all of which had degenerated more or less since that time when our first ancestors were expelled from the Garden of Eden— an event they accepted as historical fact. But Morton endorsed a theory called *polygenism,* or *multiple origins,* which argued that each of the five races was created separately and unequally at the beginning of history. This was a provocative position in the 1830s—not because of its open racism, of course, but because it contradicted the biblical pronouncement that Adam and Eve were the parents of all humankind.

For taking what he considered a principled and courageous stand in favor of reason against religious dogma, Morton believed that he was following in the tradition of heroic dissenters, like Galileo, whose theories of astronomy led him afoul of the

Inquisition. This tragic gulf between Morton's self-perception and the actual thrust of his work is what makes him so intriguing, even poignant, a figure. Despite the obvious racism of his work, Morton never saw himself as a racist ideologue but always as a progressive intellectual.

In his defense, Morton's views on race were not far out of step with his time, place, and . . . *uh* . . . race. While it is true that during the 1830s and 1840s the issue of slavery was threatening to split the nation, outspoken abolitionists were still considered an activist minority. As offensive as it is to us today, Morton's personal racism mirrored that of a plurality of Americans on what we might today call the center-right: He disliked slavery, but thought abolition was a dangerously radical idea; he implicitly assumed the superiority of the white race, but thought that personal character counted for more than racial background.

Unlike the era's outright apologists for slavery, Morton did not approach the subject of race with a preformulated list of philosophical or religious rationalizations that he was seeking to justify. To the contrary, he always claimed to work with scrupulous scientific detachment and maintained that he arrived at his racist conclusions only after being led there by the objective measurements he took.

This sounded like elaborate self-deception to many critics, including the modern-day evolutionary biologist and science historian Stephen Jay Gould, who took Morton to task in the 1980s. However, a 2011 study from the University of Pennsylvania concluded that Morton's measurements were indeed as accurate as he had asserted. This put to rest the accusation that Morton cooked his books, either consciously or not, to favor his fellow Caucasians. But the report was hardly a vindication; it merely shifted the blame from bias or faulty data to sample size and flawed postulates.

A Fashionable Skullduggery

The trickle-down form of the craniometry that Morton practiced was *phrenology,* a pseudoscience that attempted to identify irregularities in skull shapes with specific personality traits. Warmly embraced by the general public, in much the same way that pop-psychology and self-help books are today, phrenological speculation went well beyond the scientific evidence and sometimes ignored it altogether.

To parse the mysterious workings of human character, phrenologists employed a dizzying array of idiosyncratic terms such as *amativeness, philoprogenitiveness, veneration, adhesiveness,* and *wonder*—words that sounded impressive but were scientifically meaningless.

If the phrenologists' lexicon was obscure, their signature *phrenological charts* were easy enough to apprehend. You've certainly seen them before, as they are now icons of steampunk kitsch: pen and ink illustrations of heads in profile, gentlemen with stiff collars and waxed moustaches, whose hairless pates are overwritten with blobby outlines of hypothetical subregions of the brain, each captioned with the name of the characterological trait it supposedly governs. Phrenological charts were wildly popular and continued to be produced well into the twentieth century.

Physicians for the most part were never enthusiastic supporters of phrenology, but they tolerated it initially, if for no other reason than it helped popularize the medical view that the mind was the expression of a physical organ and not a metaphysical soul. But by the mid-nineteenth century, the scientific consensus had swung decisively against phrenology, and the dubious pursuit was permanently demoted to the status of a parlor trick, like palm reading or spirit tapping.

Though Morton was never a full-fledged phrenologist, he had ties to the fad, for it was his misfortune to live out his professional life during the decades when phrenology wielded its greatest influence. In particular, *George Combe*, a cofounder of the Edinburgh Phrenology Society and a public lecturer, whose tours across Europe and the United States did much to popularize the new field, was an enthusiastic promoter of Morton and tried to affiliate himself with research that he thought legitimated the principles of phrenology.

American Headhunter

In 1839, Morton decided to present to the public the results of his craniological research in a most ambitious way. His proposed book, *Crania Americana; Or, a Comparative View of the Skulls of Various Aboriginal Nations of North America: To Which Is Prefixed an Essay on the Varieties of the Human Species*, would be a work even more monumental than its title. Featuring seventy-one life-sized lithographs of skulls from his collection, beautifully rendered and painstakingly accurate, the book was intended not only to advance Morton's idea's about the relative merits of the human races but to showcase the cultural sophistication of his native Philadelphia, where the book was produced. The book sold for the unheard-of price of $20, or about $500 in today's money.

In addition to Morton's own essay on race, *Crania Americana* included an appendix on phrenology by George Combe. Combe's contribution underscored the relationship between Morton's rigorous craniometry and the more free-wheeling and speculative field of phrenology, and did much to undermine Morton's credibility with later generations of scientists.

Wagering that *Crania Americana* would make both his reputation and his fortune, Morton paid for the first edition out of his own pocket—something the chronically underfunded naturalist could ill afford.

To Morton's chagrin, his book sold very poorly. But the one place it did sell was the antebellum South, where increasingly defensive slave owners were receptive to any idea that could dress up their arbitrary privilege in the clothes of scientific inevitability. The fact that Morton was a Northerner living in a free state and that his work was so ostentatiously impartial—so *scientific*—made it that much more attractive to them to use as political propaganda.

Morton's second book, *Crania Ægyptiaca* of 1844, was far less ambitious than his debut publication. It was shorter and less lavishly illustrated than *Crania Americana;* but it conveyed a more overtly racist message (namely that ancient Egypt followed the same pattern as the US, with lighter-skinned masters rightfully enslaving naturally inferior black Africans), and it sold much better—again in the South, where it cemented Morton's reputation as a champion of the white race.

When Morton died seven years later, the *Charleston Medical Journal* laid this rancid laurel on his tomb: "We can only say that we of the South should consider him as our benefactor, for aiding most materially in giving the negro his true position as an inferior race."

Not With a Bang, But a Whimper

Shortly before his death, Morton's friends pooled their money and, in an act of thinly disguised charity, purchased his skull collection for $4,000. They donated it to the nearby Philadelphia Academy of Natural Sciences, which continued to build the collection. By the 1870s, it comprised more than 1,200 human skulls.

But then something changed. The glamour of skull-gathering suddenly evaporated. On one hand, physicians were setting crania aside and instead **poking and prodding directly at brains**, while anthropologists were now speaking about peoples in terms of language groups, like Sino-Tibetan and Indo-European. In both the hard and the soft sciences, Blumenbach's taxonomy of race was starting to feel clumsy and dated.

In 1892, the Academy sent forty-four of its skulls to the Columbian Historical Exposition in Madrid, which was commemorating the quadricentennial of the discovery of the New World. The display took third prize. When the Spanish government returned the crated skulls afterward, no one bothered unpacking them.

Morton's skulls remained in storage until the mid-1960s, when the Academy decided to opt out entirely of the business of warehousing human remains. It passed the Morton Collection on to the University of Pennsylvania, where it still resides, accessible only to researchers and only by appointment.

Among the few people today who know about Samuel Morton, there is a much repeated joke, which goes: Morton *would* have been the father of North American physical anthropology . . . if only he'd had any descendants. Through a masterful use of social diplomacy, Morton assembled a major scientific collection; he produced a beautiful book that was a tribute to Philadelphia as a center of science and culture; he set standards and procedures for cranial measuring, some of which endure to this day; and he made an early and bold attempt to scientifically describe the family of humankind.

But Morton was on the wrong side of history and of the facts. A combination of scientific advances and the exposure over time of the moral and intellectual bankruptcy of scientific racism have today plunged Morton and his collection into obscurity, if not ignominy.

See also:
Poking . . . at brains: Wilder Brain Collection, New York

View the Vomit Express

WHAT: World's largest human centrifuge

WHERE: Johnsville Centrifuge and Science Museum (aka Dynamic Flight Simulator Building), Human Centrifuge Building, Warminster

Revisit the heady days of the Space Race when the Future beckoned to the bold, the sky was never the limit, and human safety, like money, was never an object.

In the late 1940s, when the mad scientists and cowboy test pilots who would later form the core of the space program set out to break the sound barrier, it took some pencil pusher back in D.C. to wonder whether it would be safe to accelerate someone so quickly. The answer that Washington got: *Let's spin someone really fast and see.*

Enter the Johnsville human centrifuge, a mighty apparatus of steel and concrete housed in an 11,000-square-foot building. Back in the day, it was devoted solely to one purpose: spinning people *really* fast. Dangling from the end of the centrifuge's 50-foot-long arm is a 6-by-10-foot gondola. A subject is strapped in place, and a 4,000-horsepower engine spins the arm to simulate the force of a rocket accelerating. The device can revolve at speeds in excess of 170 mph, which generates more than 40 g's of force at the end of the arm. The whole machine weighs 180 tons, and when construction started, no one even knew how much it would cost.

From the time it opened in 1950 until it took its final turn in 1996, the Johnsville centrifuge helped set endurance records, recorded data that enabled engineers to design spacecraft that wouldn't kill their passengers, and made an awful lot of good astronauts awfully, *awfully* sick. Astronaut (and later senator) John Glenn called the machine *dreaded* and *sadistic*. Apollo 11 astronaut Michael Collins said it was *diabolical*. All the Mercury, Gemini, and Apollo astronauts as well as the first space shuttle crews trained at Johnsville, and they all hated it.

But crippling motion sickness wasn't the only discomfort anyone daring the centrifuge had to face. Under liftoff g-forces, a 180-pound astronaut weighs more than 500 pounds. With all that weight pressing down, it's difficult to do anything, even inhale. Trainees at the centrifuge had to learn how to breathe and how to control their movements under high-gravity conditions.

At 8 g's, you will pass out after a few seconds. Forty g's kills. A monument to engineering for its own sake and the giddy overambition of the postwar era, the Johnsville centrifuge could go well beyond lethal force. It was overkill in every sense of the word.

And there were plenty of people willing to test its capacity and their own. In 1958, two astronauts in training managed to withstand nearly a minute of intensive acceleration, peaking at 20 g's. When someone hypothesized that immersion in water might act as insulation against g-forces, it was no problem finding someone to volunteer to hold his breath and take a 31.25-g spin—a world record that still stands. That's just the way it was back then. The test pilot probably downed a double Manhattan beforehand, and grabbed a Lucky Strike on the way out.

Of course, all that acceleration insults the brain with oxygen and blood deprivation, which causes all sorts of mood disorders, like euphoria, anxiety, and confusion. It can also cause swelling in extremities, blood clots, and even a collapsed lung or a busted rib. But that's the sort of towel-snapping hazing these test pilots shrugged off.

We mere modern mortals may not be able to fill the shoes of these titans, but if you visit the Johnsville centrifuge, you *can* stand in the traces of their barf.

Go to **nadcmuseum.org** for visiting information.

New York

"This Ain't Your Grandmother's Antique Shop"

WHAT: Obscura Antiques & Oddities

WHERE: New York City

At first, it might look like any well-stocked, funky antique shop. There's the rack of vintage clothing, the sepia tone photographs and tinted postcards, the red-bound books with cracked spines. But something is off. Perhaps it is the abundance of creepy Victorian dolls, or the display case of vintage dental tools—and that can't be a *real* human head in the bell jar over by the monkey's paw ashtray, can it?

Welcome to Obscura Antiques & Oddities—with the accent on *oddities*. Offering only the finest and rarest in bizarre finds, this store, now in its third and largest East Village location, is a mecca for connoisseurs of the curious. Its one-of-a-kind artifacts have also struck a dramatic note on off-Broadway stages and added a pungent zest to the window displays of Manhattan's hippest boutiques.

On any given visit, you will be greeted by a Noah's Ark of

taxidermy mounts and jarred medical specimens; exquisite antique vials, whose delicate blue coloring indicated poison within; a bucket full of assorted pre-owned dentures; menacing **urethral irrigators**, with distended tips molded from Victorian-era rubber mellowed with age to a fine copper color; and the toothy jawbone of some killer fish, gaping in a welcoming smile. On a good day you might get to ogle a stuffed two-headed piglet, lounging stiffly amid a bower of plastic leaves and flowers, or be enlightened by a wax head that shows you what your nose will look like in thirty years if you don't treat your syphilis.

In 1997, Obscura founder Mike Zohn traded in his day job to pursue what he really cared about: collecting old, weird stuff that he could sell—so he could buy *more* old, weird stuff. Zohn's taste tends toward spooky, old-timey Americana: circus and sideshow memorabilia, taxidermy, mummies, fossils, and other natural history items—items that evoke images of freak shows, carnival barkers, and traveling medicine show swindlers. He can also tell you lots about baseball and guns.

Co-owner Evan Michelson, a onetime performance artist who also played in a succession of underground bands with names like *Killer Weasel*, brings a gothic sensibility to the partnership. Her sweet spot is the twilight realm where science and art overlap and beauty intersects with terror. She is a connoisseur of medical models, wax heads, and fancy birdcages, and is an authority on Victorian **mourning hair art**. She also swoons for a good coffin.

Michelson is a former scholar in residence at the **Morbid Anatomy Library**, a Brooklyn-based lecture hall and salon for all things strange, where she still holds occasional talks about her eclectic passions.

Don't let their sinister interests daunt: Evan and Mike are two of the friendliest New Yorkers you'll ever meet. If you ask nicely, Mike might even show you his prized medical oddity, a softball-sized human gallstone.

Go to **www.obscuraantiques.com** for more information.

See also:
Mourning hair art: Leila's Hair Museum, Missouri
Morbid Anatomy Library, New York
Urethral irrigators: Dough-Boy Prophylactic, Ohio

It's *Terribly* Lovely

WHAT: Anthropomorphic taxidermy

WHERE: Morbid Anatomy Library,
Proteus Gowanus, Brooklyn

A taxidermied mouse
enjoying waffles

Gowanus, a not-yet-gentrified neighborhood of auto body shops, dilapidated warehouses, and casket companies (*no joke!*), takes its name from Brooklyn's Gowanus Canal. Contaminated with the toxic runoff from a century of unregulated Victorian industry, this national Superfund site is so polluted today you wouldn't even want to spit into it. Nevertheless, the turgid waters of the Gowanus, flashing between sewage

A taxidermied mouse overindulging in spirits

gray and antifreeze Day-Glo as they flow past the brick and rusty-iron shoreline, possess an undeniable, haunting beauty.

A block east of the canal is where you will find the Morbid Anatomy Library. The founder and librarian is designer and self-identified dilettante Joanna Ebenstein. Since the days when she taught herself the art of taxidermy as a tween, by practicing on roadkill and other "found" objects, Ebenstein has fashioned a life for herself out of finding beauty in the macabre.

The library, which is private but open to the public, is the direct outgrowth of Ebenstein's extensive explorations of institutions like the **Mütter Museum** and the **National Museum of Health and Medicine**, as well as their older and odder European counterparts, like Florence's **La Specola**, and of her evangelizing zeal to introduce the strange seduction of anatomical art to a wider public.

Stepping into the closet-sized Morbid Anatomy Library is like walking into an old **cabinet of curiosities**. Every available surface is covered with medical displays, taxidermy mounts, seashells, pickled lizards, insect cases, devotional artifacts, miscellaneous junk culled from the street, and Ebenstein's own fine

art photographs of sensuous and ghastly **anatomical Venuses**—
all jumbled together without any plan and without apology.

The books themselves constitute a small but highly special-
ized collection focused on medical and museum history (and the
delightful subfield of circuses and freak shows), anatomical illustration, and philosophical musings on the phenomenon of
collecting and the impulse to collect. There's also some fun stuff
on sexuality and death, because . . . well, *why not?*

The Morbid Anatomy Library is part of larger, communal
project called *Observatory,* which is a sort of cross between an art
gallery, a community center, and an eighteenth-century salon,
where artists, writers, academics, and ordinary people with extraordinary hobbies gather to share their obsessions with a sym-
pathetic audience.

One of the most popular Observatory events is an occasional
class taught by a local expert on the almost-lost art of *anthropomorphic taxidermy,* or stuffing animals and mounting them in
human poses.

This vestige of Victoriana swept the English-speaking world
in 1851 with a display by the German taxidermist *Hermann
Ploucquet* at the Crystal Palace Exhibition, which was the world's
first World's Fair. Although Ploucquet worked for the Royal Museum in Stuttgart, it was his whimsical *mountings* (that's what
you call a piece of taxidermy, a *mounting*) of animals re-creating
scenes from German fables that charmed the public—including
Victoria herself, who recollected Ploucquet's display in her diary
as "really marvellous."

Typical anthropomorphic taxidermy pieces were small tableaux of two to four animals, whose incongruous humor lay in
their mimicking quintessentially human activities. There were

displays of mouse boxers and frog swordsmen, cigarette-smoking hares and pipe-smoking squirrels, and ferret schoolmasters disciplining recalcitrant bunny pupils. These pieces are part of a rich tradition of worldly-wise animals that starts with Aesop's fables and ends, on one side, with the genius that is Bugs Bunny, and the ignominy of dogs-playing-poker art, on the other.

The master of anthropomorphic taxidermy was the Englishman Walter Potter, whose work in the late nineteenth and early twentieth centuries took the craft to unimagined heights. Potter's sweeping dioramas, which typically range from 3 feet to 2 yards in length, featured painted backdrops, simulated landscaping, and model houses complete with toy furniture. They also could contain dozens of taxidermy animals, all dressed in tiny costumes. *The Kitten's Croquet Party*, for instance, arrays thirty-seven felines sipping tea on the lawn of a country estate, lounging beneath parasols, riding tiny bicycles, and wielding kitten-sized croquet mallets. Potter's tour de force, *The Death and Burial of Cock Robin*, employed ninety-eight bird specimens to depict the eerie nursery rhyme.

While taxidermy mounts are often referred to as *stuffed animals*, that is actually a misnomer. *Taxi-dermy* literally means *moved-skin*. Rather than emptying out the soft, fleshy parts of the specimen and refilling the husk of a carcass with something more resistant to decay—as the term *stuffed animal* implies—taxidermists actually remove the skin and treat it before placing it on a cast replica of the original animal.

It takes great artistry to make a convincing taxidermy mount, and throughout the nineteenth century, anthropomorphic taxidermists honed their technique right alongside their more conventional peers. While naturalist-artists at upstate New York's **Ward's Natural Science Establishment** were mounting specimens to supply the nation's burgeoning natural history museums, lower-brow venues like Scudder's Museum in Lower Manhattan (which P. T. Barnum eventually acquired and turned into his American Museum) offered more spurious but crowd-pleasing displays like putative mermaids and unicorns or tableaux of amorous dogs courting demure cats.

The popularity of anthropomorphic taxidermy dwindled away by the mid-twentieth century—partially because people's attitude toward animals had changed, and partially because, in the age of modernism, holdovers from the Victorian era just seemed shabby and weird.

But in many circles today, shabby and weird is A-OK. In Brooklyn and other hipster enclaves across the country, this twee handicraft with a gothic edge is enjoying a second life. (Speaking of life, it should be noted that the taxidermy classes at Observatory use only feeder mice otherwise destined for snakes and lizards. No animal is killed specifically for Art.)

If you'd like to tour the Morbid Anatomy Library, lobby for more anthropomorphic taxidermy classes, or see what Observatory lectures are upcoming, visit **morbidanatomy.blogspot.com**.

See also:
Anatomical Venuses, La Specola: Medical Venus, Kentucky
Cabinets of curiosities: Ward's Natural Science Establishment, New York
Mütter Museum, Pennsylvania
National Museum of Health and Medicine, Washington, D.C.

Absence Makes the Dong Grow Longer

WHAT: The reproductive equipage
of Semibalanus balanoides

WHERE: Long Island Sound, Long Island

There are some venues that are simply not conducive to the art of love—hammocks, for instance, or inflatable rafts. A more stable but seemingly no less insurmountable arrangement would have you rooted in one spot and your love-object firmly planted, say, fifty or sixty feet away.

That scenario, however, is business as usual for *Semibalanus balanoides,* or the *acorn barnacle—*aka *the just regular barnacle.* (In a marvelously unilluminating piece of nomenclature, the scientific name of this species means *half-acorn thing that looks like an acorn.*)

What geography hath put asunder, in the case of the acorn barnacle, nature hath found means to join together: These plucky little crustaceans have evolved the longest penises of any creature relative to body size.

Acorn barnacles dwell in shallow waters and tidal zones, stuck fast to rocks, ship hulls, and other hard, flat surfaces, where they contend with limpets and mussels in a life-or-death struggle for territory that is exceptionally slow-moving and boring to watch.

Barnacles are born free-swimming, but when a juvenile finds a nice homey spot, it attaches itself to the surface, using adhesive secreted from glands near its antennae to cement itself in a permanent headstand. The immobile barnacle then feeds by extending its legs and grabbing at plankton that float within reach.

For mutual protection, barnacles grow together in colonies. Sometimes they are packed cheek by jowl (or would be, if they *had* cheeks and jowls rather than armor plates and not much else). In other instances, the clusters can be thinner and spread out.

To accommodate for this geographic variability, each male barnacle grows a penis that is custom fitted for his neighborhood. Where lady barnacles are few and far between, a male will grow a penis with many dark *annulations*—or *ring folds*—that can stretch out like a vacuum cleaner hose, up to eight times the owner's body size! (Before you get all a-titter, ladies, that works out only to about 2.5 inches, or 64 millimeters. Barnacles are shrimpy things.) In tighter quarters, barnacles will conserve their strength and make do with something more modest. It's safer too: Longer appendages are apt to snap off in stormy seas.

These prurient biological facts were all confirmed in a study conducted off the shores of Long Island Sound in 2005. By the way, no barnacles were harmed in that experiment. Since barnacles grow new sex organs each mating season anyway, researchers were essentially collecting last season's castoffs.

The Original Brain In a Vat

WHAT: Wilder Brain Collection

WHERE: Cornell University, Ithaca

Dr. Burt Green Wilder was Cornell's first animal biologist and the founder of the university's anatomy department. But among today's undergraduates passing by the display case outside the psychology department in Uris Hall, he's better recognized as the fourth brain from the right.

Dr. Wilder's disembodied brain—soaking in a jar of gold-tinged formaldehyde and flanked by seven companions, identified as three fellow professors, two former students, a suffragette, and one intriguing fellow simply labeled "**a gentleman, scholar, and murderer**"—is a sample from the shelves of the eponymous Wilder Brain Collection, the first repository of its kind in the nation and the . . . *er* . . . brainchild of this pioneering figure in neuroscience.

At its peak, Dr. Wilder's collection comprised more than six hundred human brains and hundreds more animal samples. But these were not just any brains. A tireless booster who even went so far as to distribute organ bequest forms at alumni dinners, Wilder persuaded, cajoled, and flattered scores of the intellectual elite to leave him their brains once they had finished with them. A true believer in his enterprise, when Wilder died in 1925, he donated his own brain to the collection.

The purpose of the massive headhunt was to test whether the brains of "educated and orderly persons"—Wilder's own words—were measurably different from those of everybody else. Now you might think that sounds horrifically classist—and it does—but in the terms of his age, Wilder was one of the good guys. In fact, he was a decent man by any standard.

Like most other scientists of his day, Wilder seriously entertained the proposition that science could be used to improve the human race—not just increase its comforts and raise its capacity to achieve, but improve the *actual* human race, by applying to ourselves the same principles that allow us to breed meatier chickens and milkier cows.

That's *eugenics* in a nutshell, and it is a very, *very* unpopular idea today. But of course, we have the example of history's most infamous eugenicist, Adolf Hitler, to look back on, and people of

Wilder's day did not. From the 1880s to the 1930s, eugenics actually seemed an enlightened, progressive idea, and it was popular with social reformers, who thought the concept implied nothing more than the brightest minds using objective science to promote the healthiest society. Cynics that we are today, there is not a single premise in that statement that we would not question. And that's a good thing, too.

Wilder believed that some people were inherently better than others, and it was his scientific quest to find the physical source of that moral inequality. But to his great credit, Wilder understood that science and scientists did not always meet their ideal of impartiality. He was an outspoken critic of the **scientific racism** that tainted the work of earlier skull collectors and some proponents of eugenics. Throughout his life, in fact, Wilder was convinced that, as far as race was concerned, there was less there than met the eye: Skin color, head shape, and facial features could tell us nothing about an individual's character. For Wilder, that secret lay deeper.

Brothers in Arms; Equals in Death

Wilder launched his collection in 1889, but the germ of the idea may have been planted decades earlier when he served as a surgeon during the Civil War.

Wilder had been attached to the 55th Massachusetts Volunteer Infantry, which was just the second regiment to be formed of African-American enlisted men. You can see an excellent representation of what army life must have been like for Wilder's men in the 1989 movie *Glory*, which dramatizes the story of the 54th, the first black regiment. Joining a black unit as a white officer was a sign of a particular commitment to abolition and was itself an act of courage. If captured, officers in black units risked summary execution by Southern soldiers; and these units were not particularly popular with Northern troops either, who may have been fighting for abolition in the abstract but often felt no particular affection for real, live African-Americans. The black soldiers of the 54th and 55th were chronically undersupplied and repeatedly denied the same pay as their white compatriots. In his wartime memoirs, Wilder describes his troops as spending more time facing down Northern prejudice than Southern guns.

As a battlefield physician, Wilder had had ample opportunity to get close to human brains in all their squishy physicality—closer perhaps than he wanted. But in later life, Wilder also described being deeply moved by the acts of transcendent courage and gallantry he had seen displayed on the battlefield. Wilder's firsthand observation of men stripped to their moral core by the exigencies of suffering and terror started the young physician to wondering just where in the body that moral center might lie and what signs—if any—below the surface of the skin might reveal the quality of a person's character or differentiate one race from another.

To Wilder, as to most other scientists of the day, the answer seemed to lie in the architecture of the brain. The accepted hypothesis was that somewhere in the folds and contours of that organ lay the secret to what distinguished the genius from the lunatic, the poet from the cretin, and the hero from the criminal.

Today the idea looks perilously close to palm reading, but in the very early days of neuroscience, it was the best hypothesis going. And it marked an improvement from **craniometry**, which, in essence, was an attempt to correlate intellectual capacity to skull size. Researchers around the world, from Paris to Moscow to Tokyo, were taking calipers and scales to whatever brains they could lay hands on and starting to crunch the numbers.

A Pyrrhic Victory

As the nineteenth century ended, however, it became increasingly clear that simply measuring brain shape was also a scientific dead end. By his retirement in 1910, Wilder admitted that his investigation had been a failure: No meaningful differences in brain structure could be detected with the tools of his day.

But for Wilder, the failure was only partial. The absence of correlation between brain shape and personality demolished in Wilder's view any scientific basis for claiming an innate intellectual inequality between the races.

Work continued on with Wilder's collection into the twentieth century, but without the earlier enthusiasm. Ironically, the cancerous flower of scientific racism blossomed once again, and it was Nazism's embrace of eugenics that destroyed once and for all the credibility of craniometry and brain collecting. To the public eye, Wilder's project was equally suspect. During World War II the collection quietly stopped accepting contributions. Wilder's experiment was over for good.

The collection languished through the decades, and by the 1970s many of the specimens had seriously decayed. Cornell was ready to donate what remained to the Smithsonian as a scientific oddity, when a young psychology professor took an interest in this historic, if unsuccessful, foray into brain mapping.

With the help of a team of students, Prof. Barbara Finlay pruned the once mighty collection down to just about seventy healthy brains and moved them into the basement of Uris Hall.

They selected eight specimens of special note, and put them on display near the psychology department.

What remains of Dr. Wilder's collection is now less a functioning scientific apparatus than an admonition, a sort of *memento mori*—or, more accurately, *memento corporis*: a stark reminder of the physicality of the brain, and a challenge for young students of the mind to face the fact that, whatever our intellectual pretensions, we too amount to little more than brains in vats. As Dr. Finlay told the *New York Times*, "The students who come in here and pass by the display cabinet are forced to confront the brain. This is the thing. This is where you happen."

See also:

Craniometry, Scientific racism: Morton skull collection, Pennsylvania

"Gentleman, scholar, and murderer": Rulloff's Bar, New York

Preserved brains: Ward's Natural Science Establishment, New York

Brainiac or Maniac?

WHAT: Rulloff's Bar

WHERE: Ithaca, New York

One thing about college kids, they sure love to drink—flights of microbrews, margaritas served in fishbowls, and unwholesome blends of random spirits branded with names that end in *tini*. They also seem to think that murderers and diners are a natural pairing. [See: **The Alferd Packer Grill, Colorado**]

That can be the only explanation for the success of Rulloff's

Bar. This Collegetown food 'n' grog fixture, located literally across the street from Cornell University, takes its name from Edward H. Rulloff, who for a short time in the late nineteenth century was the most famous scholar in New York's Southern Tier region . . . because he was also the most infamous murderer in New York's Southern Tier region.

Entirely self-educated, this son of German immigrants was conversant in chemistry, philosophy, and law. Without a credential to his name, Rulloff worked as a teacher, then as a physician, and presented a paper on linguistics to the American Philological Association.

Rulloff was also a career criminal, who taught himself the seven languages he needed to write his philological address while he was in jail. It is almost a certainty that he murdered his wife and young daughter, but he hid the bodies so well that he escaped justice. Rulloff was finally run to ground in 1871, when he was convicted for murdering a Binghamton clerk during a botched robbery.

Exuding an aura of danger as well as good-natured, masculine bonhomie, the murderer Rulloff was nearly an object of hero worship to the army of newspapermen sent to cover his trial— including Mark Twain, who wrote an editorial imploring some noble soul to come forward as a gallows surrogate, à la *A Tale of Two Cities,* and save this singular intellect from the hangman's noose.

According to Rulloff's the bar, Rulloff the man's last words were "Hurry it up! I want to be in hell in time for dinner." Other sources claim more prosaically that the bound and hooded prisoner's last earthly deed was to gripe, "I can't stand still."

After his execution, Rulloff's brain was transferred to Cornell's **Wilder Brain Collection**, a coveted prize from a donor equally brilliant *and* disordered. Wilder himself studied the organ and proclaimed it the largest he had ever observed.

See also:
The Wilder Brain Collection, New York

Specimens Served Under Glass

WHAT: Ward's Natural Science Establishment

WHERE: Rochester

An example of a wet specimen— the classic frog in jar

Those sinister "wet specimens" locked in cupboards at the back of every high-school biology classroom—the ubiquitous bullfrog, the infamous fetal pig, the soul-wrenching preserved cat—ghastly and contorted in their glass prisons, may look as though they had been lifted directly from a *Saw* movie set. Chances are, however, that they actually came from an ordinary-looking warehouse in upstate New York.

Ward's Natural Science Establishment, founded in 1862, is one of the nation's oldest and largest suppliers of science education apparatus. Among its wares, you will find skeletons of people (fake) and animals (real), bugs in display cases, novelty tarantula paperweights and insect keychains, forensic equipment for honing fingerprinting and hair analysis skills, and—*la pièce de résistance*—preserved specimens. In addition to the pickled delicacies already mentioned above, Ward's offers sheep's brains, earthworms, eels, a variety of lower orders, such as lichens and algae, as well as a cheerful creature called *the sea peach*.

Being the foremost supplier of ghoulish lab accessories that have traumatized generation after generation of unwilling sophomore biologists is, however, only the latest chapter in Ward's 150-year story.

He-Man Natural History

Three hundred years ago, natural history was the province of a peculiar breed of gentleman-collector. This was the sort of fellow who would fund an expedition to the Amazon out of his own pocket, endure the hardships of crossing the tempestuous Atlantic in a sailing ship, suffer through recurrent bouts of dysentery and malaria, and rebuff assaults from wild animals and the occasional hostile tribe of indigenous people simply to experience the satisfaction of setting up an easel and painting watercolor portraits of beetles and pampas grasses no European had seen before.

If they survived to return home, these two-fisted naturalists would display their souvenirs in hodgepodge collections they called *cabinets of curiosities*. In these private galleries you might see—in no particular order—taxidermy dodos next to pieces of coral and uncut gemstones, blowguns from Guiana, dinosaur fossils from Devon, classical statuary, European oil paintings, wooden clubs from the Philippines inset with jagged sharks' teeth, volcanic stones, meteorites—whatever natural oddities and human *objets d'art* had struck the fancy of the collector.

Born in 1834, Henry Augustus Ward, the founder of Ward's Natural Science Establishment, was part of the generation of naturalists that would transform the study of nature from a dilettantish hobby into a scientific discipline. An avid fossil collector from childhood, Ward was inspired by the great European cabinets of curiosities to assemble collections of his own.

Like his forebears, he, too, was something of an Indiana Jones—he traversed sandstorms in the Sinai, caught smallpox in Africa, and shot big game on the prairie with his friend Buffalo Bill Cody.

Unlike his predecessors, though, Ward and his contemporaries had been exposed to Darwin's ideas about evolution through natural selection. Equipped with a more systematic and scientifically rigorous tool for classifying animals and plants than earlier specimen hunters, they took the idiosyncratic, if charming, cabinet of curiosity and made it into the modern museum.

Through his Natural Science Establishment, Henry A. Ward assembled a team that scoured the world for natural curiosities—animal, vegetable, and mineral—that workers back in the Rochester studio would stuff, pickle, and otherwise preserve and display. Ward then sold these collections to museums throughout the country. His most prestigious project would be assembling the core of Chicago's natural history museum, now known as the Field Museum.

As museums became more established, they were increasingly able to handle their own acquisition and taxidermy needs and no longer needed a middleman like Ward's to do it for them. At the same time, however, high school science classes, which were also responding to Darwin, were beginning to incorporate modern biology into the curriculum. By the 1920s, there was a large classroom demand for specimens to study and dissect, and Ward's was there to fill it.

The Secret to Immortality

Today Ward's employs a variety of preservation methods depending on the type of specimen and its classroom purpose.

Insects and other very simple creatures not destined for the dissection knife are simply dropped, still living, into alcohol—voilà, specimen!

With higher animals, things are more complicated. Frogs, for example, get a preliminary soak in benzocaine, a mild pain reliever used in cough drops and earwax treatments for people. Fished out from their anesthetic bath either dead or senseless, the amphibians are transferred to a vat of formalin solution—a less toxic form of the embalming fluid formaldehyde—that *fixes* the tissue, preventing it from decomposing. Colored latex is injected into the blood system to make arteries and veins easier to see. The frogs are then put in a barrel of preservative and left to cure before being packaged for delivery.

The most unsettling preservation method, though, might be freeze-drying, which removes all the water from a specimen through freezing in a vacuum at very low temperatures. (Think of it as *serious* freezer burn.) When you receive your freeze-dried grass frog, just remove it from its storage pouch, drop it into an alcohol solution to rehydrate, and it's good as new! Except for the still-being-dead part.

A Fitting End

Henry Ward died in 1906. (A final landmark in an eventful life, Ward, who was struck by a car, was Rochester's first automobile fatality.) In a most appropriate legacy, Ward's brain was removed and presented to his friend and colleague Dr. Burt Green Wilder, and became itself a specimen in the **Wilder Brain Collection** at Cornell University.

See also:
Wilder Brain Collection, New York
The Field Museum, Chicago

Uncle Sam Went Here

WHAT: Chamber pot belonging to Samuel Wilson, aka Uncle Sam

WHERE: Rensselaer County Historical Society, Troy

When he was just a boy, Samuel Wilson and his family left their home in Menotomy, Massachusetts (now known as *Arlington*), and moved to Mason, New Hampshire. In 1789, at the age of twenty-two, Wilson set out to make a life for himself. Crossing out of New England, he settled in Troy, New York, a recently formed community on the eastern banks of the Hudson River. The enterprising young man took a turn at a variety of trades—bricklaying, distilling, farming. By the early 1790s, Wilson had taken up cattle slaughtering, a job at which he excelled.

By 1797, Wilson had prospered enough to return to Mason and claim his sweetheart, Betsey Mann, whom he brought back with him to Troy. Betsey eventually bore Samuel four children. In a few years, Wilson was employing two hundred men at two slaughterhouses, which, according to an advertisement in the local paper from 1805, could "kill, cut, and pack 150 head of cattle per day."

Samuel Wilson died at the venerable age of eighty-seven, a respected and well-liked member of the community. Indeed, his kindliness was so marked throughout his life that he had been universally called *Uncle Sam*—sometimes even by his own children.

He did not have a goatee. He never wore red-and-white striped pants. And, although he did own a top hat, it was most certainly *not* emblazoned with stars and stripes. It was just ordinary beaver felt. But, by an act of Congress, Samuel Wilson of Troy, New York, is the original Uncle Sam.

How did this humble Hudson Valley meatpacker become the mascot of the world's oldest and most powerful republic? The story begins with the War of 1812. As the nation was mobilizing for war, Wilson was subcontracted through a man named Elbert Anderson, Jr., to provision troops stationed downriver in the town of Greenbush. That much can be verified; it's the next part that starts to take on the cast of an urban legend. The barrels of meat that Wilson packed for the army were supposedly marked *E.A.—U.S.* standing for *From Elbert Anderson, to the United States Government*. When some anonymous quartermaster on the receiving end of a shipment asked Wilson's men what the label stood for, a sportive teamster is said to have replied, "I'm sure I don't know, sir, unless it means Elbert Anderson and Uncle Sam Wilson!" The Yankee soldiers, evidently easily amused, henceforth took to cleverly "misreading" *US* as *Uncle Sam*.

How much of that story is *really* true? Did Wilson really

address his cargo with the enigmatic ciphers *E.A.—U.S.*? Did a noncommissioned officer in the United States Army really not know what the initials US stood for? Would some wiseass from upstate really sass a federal representative? Well, one out of three does not make for a compelling case.

At any rate, Congress passed a resolution, so now the story is *officially* true, whatever the *actual* facts are.

And those actual facts are ambiguous. A hundred years ago, a certain Albert Mathews combed over hundreds of newspaper articles and other cultural ephemera to compile the earliest source materials on Uncle Sam. You can read his exhaustive paper in the *Proceedings of the American Antiquarian Society, New Series, Vol. XIX*, from 1908. (Available for free on Google books.)

According to Mathews's research, the first instance in print of Uncle Sam standing in for the US government appears in the September 7, 1813, edition of the *Troy Post*. It was a novel enough expression that the author felt the need to explain in a footnote that "Uncle Sam" was a slang expression among soldiers. Troy newspapers continued to use the nickname for decades without ever connecting it back to Sam Wilson. In fact, that story was first published by an Albany paper in 1842. It was not until 1876, twenty-two years after Wilson's death, that a native Troy publication reprinted the story.

Indeed, a *Post* article from 1816 presents an origin story that has nothing to do with Uncle Sam Wilson. A reporter talking to soldiers from the light dragoons asked what the USLD on their caps stood for. (*Duh!*) He received the facetious reply, "*Uncle Sam's Lazy Dogs.*"

But that's not the final vying Uncle Sam explanation that Mathews's research discovered. Tousled hair covered with cobwebs and blood hot from the thrill of the hunt, the dogged antiquarian goes on to speculate that Uncle Sam might be an allusion to the tenth stanza of "Yankee Doodle Dandy," as it appeared in a private edition of 1824, which claimed to be based on lyrics from 1789. But something in that hypothesis feels a little *too* close to, say, citing the Japanese bootleg of the original Basing Street demo of "Stairway to Heaven," the one without the Jimmy Page guitar overdub. It's probably as credible.

Over time, the citizens of Troy have been as undecided over their hometown hero as the facts have been. Ignoring the story at first, the town embraced it by the end of the nineteenth century. In the 1930s, they pushed for congressional recognition. In 1961, they got it. (The official statement in its entirety reads: *Resolved by the Senate and the House of Representatives that the Congress salutes Uncle Sam Wilson of Troy, New York, as the progenitor of America's National symbol of Uncle Sam.*) Then, in the early 1970s, the city of Troy bulldozed Uncle Sam's house . . . to make way for a freeway . . . that was never built.

Twenty years later, remorse set in, and the town sent archeologists to scour the remains of Uncle Sam's demolished home to unearth any Wilsonian artifacts. The most noteworthy relic from the excavation is a clay bowl about the size of a houseplant container. It's a chamber pot, and more than likely it was kept for the personal convenience of Uncle Sam himself.

The lidless bowl is plain on the inside, while the outside is divided into two large, colored bands, white above and terra-cotta below, which are framed, top and bottom, by bands of green. The colors look more ancient Roman than Colonial-era country craft. And rather than the flower or goose motifs you might expect, the pot is ornamented with two fat, ropy squiggles, which disconcertingly resemble undulating lengths of colon. The personal Porta-Potty has a wide, flat lip, out of which a bite-sized chip is missing. Otherwise the device is complete and looks as ready for service now as it was a century and a half ago.

You can see this historic chamber pot, along with other memorabilia of Uncle Sam, the man as well as the symbol, at the Rensselaer County Historical Society's permanent exhibit, *Uncle Sam: The Man in Life and Legend*. For hours and admission details, go to **www.rchsonline.org**.

Massachusetts

Better to Light One Candle Than to Curse the Dog Poop

WHAT: Park Spark poop-fueled light

WHERE: Cambridge

The Park Spark Project

We have all been told that when life gives you lemons, you should make lemonade. In a similar spirit, when life gives artist and activist Matthew Mazzotta dog poop, he makes . . . power from methane gas.

OK, that lacks a certain aphoristic ring, but it is solid advice about solid waste that we all could benefit from following.

In the spring of 2010, Mazzotta installed in a Cambridge dog park a device that naturally converts dog droppings into energy that can be used to power practically any type of gadget. In this case, it is an old-fashioned gas-burning lamppost. One part art, one part science, and one part community outreach, this installation is part of an ongoing project Mazzotta calls *Park Spark*, and it could be coming to a public space near you.

The heart of the Park Spark project is a large metal tank called a *methane digester*. An unsavory name, but apt. It does exactly what our stomach does—it *digests*, or breaks down, organic matter into a form we can extract energy from. The feces have, of course, been digested once already, but there is lots of energy in there still. When a conscientious dog owner drops a sack of doggie doo into the Park Spark digester and gives a crank a couple of turns to swish up the mess inside, hungry anaerobic bacteria set to breaking down the organic refuse. The name for the process is *anaerobic respiration*, and it takes a while to explain it in detail. But the gist is that, after a series of eatings and excretings by a zoo of microorganisms, you're left in the end with bio-sludge and energy-rich methane gas.

Methane (CH_4) is a compound of carbon and hydrogen. It is a colorless, odorless substance that is a major component of natural gas. When methane is burned to release its latent energy, each molecule breaks down into two molecules of water vapor

(H_2O) and one of carbon dioxide (CO_2). Yes, carbon dioxide is a greenhouse gas, but methane is a much, *much* worse greenhouse gas: about *30 times* more damaging to the ozone layer than CO_2.

Dog waste sent to the landfill will eventually break down into methane all on its own. But, in that case, the gas is allowed just to seep into the atmosphere. A digester, on the other hand, hurries along the process and captures the methane for later use. So by producing energy from waste *and* lowering greenhouse emissions, a digester is a double win for the environment.

Mazzotta would like to take Park Spark national, but Americans have been slow to embrace this innovation in waste-processing technology. The story is different in the rest of the world. India and China, two giant nations with outsized appetites for energy, have warmly accepted home methane digesters as a means to keep industry booming. In more laid-back northern Europe, where hippies and stoners abound, green technology is embraced more as a lifestyle choice. Before his Massachusetts project, Mazzotta built an installation at a farm in the Netherlands that uses cow manure to heat water for a teahouse.

As yet, though, the move from terrier tail to teacup might be putting methane digesters and human digestion a little too close for the taste of many Americans.

Check out the latest Park Spark projects online at **park sparkproject.com**.

You *Can* Judge This Book by Its Cover

WHAT: The memoir of George Walton, a rare
example of anthropodermic biblioplegy

WHERE: Boston Athenæum, Boston

George Walton (born James Allen, aka Jonas Pierce, aka James
H. York, aka Burley Grove) was an infamous criminal in the early
days of the republic, who haunted the forests and skulked the
hamlets near old Boston. He was a thief, a bank robber, a whore-
monger, a highwayman, an arsonist, a jailbreaker, and an attempted murderer. He was also a trained cobbler—a trade he
picked up during a two-year stretch in the state pen.

Better for Walton that he had stuck with shoes, for from
the time of his first arrest in 1824 at age fifteen, the spirited
malefactor would be tried six times, convicted four times, and
sentenced to a total of thirty-seven years, six months, and twelve
days' imprisonment, much of it in hard labor. As it turned out,
Walton would serve just ten of those years before dying in
a prison cell of consumption at the age of twenty-seven. Well,
that's *one* way of beating the rap.

All very interesting, you are probably thinking, *but where's
the gross?* True enough, there is nothing so far in the biography
of Mr. Walton-Allen-Pierce-York-Grove that would distinguish
him from a thousand other rogues and cutpurses, footpads,
whoremongers, gunslingers, and desperadoes whose depreda-
tions made the American frontier a legendarily colorful and
dangerous—if not especially gross—place.

Walton's contribution to the nation's rich heritage of all things
sick-making occurred after his death. It came in the form of a

slender book, less than fifty pages thick, that now resides in the venerable Boston Athenæum, one of the nation's oldest libraries. It is a copy of Walton's deathbed confessions, dictated from prison, set into print, and bound . . . *in human leather!*

Cute Compressa Est

Walton's confessions looks like an ordinary antique book, covered in what seems to be off-white doeskin and stitched around the edges with thick leather thongs. But a large Latin inscription set right in the cover dispels any misunderstanding:

HIC LIBER WALTONIS

CUTE COMPRESSA EST

(This book in Walton's skin is bound.)

Anthropodermic bibliopegy, or the binding of books in human skin, is a rightfully uncommon practice. Fixing a precise estimate of the number of anthropodermic books is impossible, since the morally questionable nature of these volumes encourages their owners to keep a low profile. However, it is safe to say that the number of such books in public collections is somewhere in the hundreds—a surprising number of them being discreetly tucked away in prestigious university libraries, like Harvard's Houghton and Brown's John Hay.

Embodying, as it does, a stomach-churning combination of both the most rarefied and bestial aspects of humanity, a book bound in human skin inevitably evokes associations with that period of soaring faith and exuberant savagery, the Middle Ages.

The facts, however, show that the man-skin book is actually not an artifact of medieval cruelty, but of Enlightenment science.

Most anthropodermic books are medical textbooks that date from the eighteenth and early nineteenth centuries. The anatomists, who studied the human body by cutting up cadavers obtained from prison and paupers cemeteries, often used the leftover scraps as leather binding for their lavishly illustrated books. Far from being perceived as gruesome, it seemed perfectly appropriate that a book which revealed the secrets of the human body on its *inside* should be covered by human flesh on the *outside*.

Besides, waste not, want not, right?

To be sure, however, there are at least a few examples of anthropodermic books that were terroristic rather than educational in intent. During the bloody time that followed the French Revolution, at least one copy of the newly drafted French constitution and several copies of Thomas Paine's *Rights of Man* were covered in the tanned hides of deposed aristocrats, press-ganged posthumously into the service of *Liberté, Égalité, et Fraternité*. (This is a textbook example of what your English teacher would call *situational irony*.)

Highwayman George Walton's memoir is not the only prison confession that was bound in human skin either. But it might be the only one that was made at the prisoner's own request. According to records in the Boston Athenæum, Walton stipulated that his book should be delivered to a Mr. John Fenno, a stranger whom Walton had shot in the course of a robbery. Despite his pistol wound, Fenno had found the gumption to grapple with his attacker—a unique display of courage in Walton's experience. Deeply impressed, the dying bandit bequeathed his book as tribute to the only man doughty enough to resist him.

When Fenno died, the book passed into the hands of his daughter, who was not particularly pleased with the macabre legacy. Exasperated with the way her children would use the ghoulish book to frighten other kids in the neighborhood, it was she who donated the curious piece of Americana to the Athenæum.

Sometime later, the *Boston Transcript* published a recollection of another unorthodox use the book had been put to. According to a Fenno grandson, the original owner himself had used Walton's book "in place of the family slipper, as an instrument of punishment, on the theory, probably, that the skin of a bad man was particularly adapted for warming that of a bad child."

If, at the end of his short, misspent life, George Walton had entertained any hope that his volume might prevent another soul from straying, that's probably not what he had in mind. But as we all know, there is more than one way to skin a cat.

The Boston Athenæum is a members-only institution. But anyone with Internet access can see the cover of Walton's skin book, read a transcript of his memoir, and browse through other rarities at the Athenæum on its website: **bostonathenaeum.org.**

THE FAR WEST:
Noncontiguous States

Hawai'i

Exiles in Paradise

WHAT: Kalaupapa leprosy settlement

WHERE: Kalaupapa National Historical Park, Moloka'i

**View of the Kalaupapa Settlement by
Edward Clifford ca. 1880s**

Moloka'i is the fourth of the eight major islands of Hawai'i, counting west to east. In the middle of the island is a triangular peninsula called *Kalaupapa*, which juts upward like a shark fin. The region is good farmland, whose rich volcanic soil sustains sweet potatoes, fruit, and taro that can be pounded into *poi*. But historically, Kalaupapa was never much settled. With two sides bordered by ocean and southern access to the main island cut off by the highest sea cliffs on earth—a sheer 2,000-foot rise or *pali*—Kalaupapa was just too hard to get to.

This isolation is precisely the reason that in 1865 the king of Hawai'i, Kamehameha V, chose Kalaupapa as the location to establish a permanently quarantined medical settlement. In January 1866, the first inmates, a shipload of 101 men and 41 women, arrived at Kalaupapa. All had been seized from their families and forcibly relocated; all 142 of them had been diagnosed with leprosy.

Over the next one hundred and three years, eight thousand more people with leprosy would be banished to this paradisiacal prison.

Portrait of a Killer

Leprosy is a terrible disease with an even darker history. So great was the fear and heavy the prejudice against people who suffered from leprosy that many now consider the name itself to be a dirty word, as offensive as a racial epithet. Beyond rehabilitation, that older term has been replaced by the blander designation *Hansen's disease,* after the Norwegian doctor G. H. Armauer Hansen, who in 1873 identified the source of the scourge as the microorganism *Mycrobacterium leprae.*

Hansen's disease damages the nerves in the extremities, which causes numbness in the fingers, face, and feet. As they atrophy from lack of use, the fingers and toes wither and seize up. Some patients lose the reflex to blink, and then they lose their eyesight as their corneas become damaged from prolonged exposure to dirt and sunlight. In some cases, Hansen's disease is accompanied by disfiguring growths called *tubercles,* which can cover the face, hands, and feet with warty lesions similar to **syphilitic gummas**.

Contrary to the horror stories, Hansen's disease does not actually cause body parts to drop off. But the numbness caused by nerve damage does make patients prone to self-injury. Hurt your finger enough, and it will eventually drop off—but technically, it wouldn't be the disease's fault.

A Case of Mistaken Identity

Before the advent of germ theory, disease epidemics were often attributed to divine wrath. And why not? They arose suddenly, spread inexplicably, and killed mercilessly. The Greeks of Homer's time, for example, imagined that plague victims were felled by arrows shot from the bow of Apollo, the god of pestilence. In the Judeo-Christian tradition, it was an outbreak of leprosy, among the panoply of diseases to choose from, that was the surest sign of an angry god. *Leprosy* is mentioned nearly forty times in the Bible, and if you count all its forms—like *leper* and *leprous*—the number doubles.

It is ironic, then, that the leprosy of the Bible is not the leprosy that we know today. The word in question—*tzaraath*, in the original Hebrew—means something like a *smiting* or *affliction* and, in its Old Testament context, seems to apply to a variety of skin ailments, some relatively minor. In the century following the death of Alexander the Great, the Jewish scholars in ancient Alexandria who translated Hebrew scripture into Greek coined their own word, deriving it from the verb *lepen,* which means to *scale (a fish)* or *to strip (bark).*

Thus, etymologically speaking, the word *leprosy* might originally have meant roughly the same thing as the English term
shingles, which is its own sort of skin disease. But, like the original scribes, the Greek translators evidently did not have any
particular illness in mind. If they had actually meant Hansen's
disease, they would presumably have used their own word for it,
which was *elephantiasis.*

The mix-up happened in the Middle Ages, when Hansen's disease flourished between the eleventh and thirteenth centuries.
The outbreak was so horrific that everybody assumed it must
have been a form of divine retribution. They consulted scripture
and found a malady condemned by Prophets and Church Fathers
alike which seemed to fit the present situation quite nicely, so
they called their plague *leprosy.*

Expanding on guidelines laid out in Leviticus, medieval lep-
ers were required to cover themselves entirely, so that others
would not have to look at them, and to announce their approach
by wearing signs, ringing bells, or simply shouting "Unclean!
Unclean!" Sometimes they were quarantined in leper colonies or
hospitals, where the wealthy and the lucky might find, not a
cure, but at least compassionate care. Leprosy was viewed as a
living death. Sometimes symbolic funeral services were held to
signify that social death and allow heirs to inherit property immediately.

Looking for medical advice in a book of spiritual guidance is
a misstep in reasoning that logicians call a *category error.* Since,
in the Middle Ages, there was little medical knowledge and less
that could be done to effectively treat leprosy, this was perhaps
less an error of thought than an understandable act of desper-
ation. But this conflation of a medical disease and divine judg-

ment led to nine hundred years of scapegoating people with Hansen's disease—which was already torment enough without the added burden of misdirected moral condemnation.

The medieval leprosy epidemic mysteriously burned itself out in most of Europe. Equally mysteriously, it decided to linger in Scandinavia, where Hansen's disease remained a serious health threat up to the twentieth century. For the most part, though, our ancestors sighed a collective sigh of relief . . . just in time to be decimated by the Black Death, which was about to sweep the known world in one of history's deadliest pandemics.

But that is another story.

Blue Hawai'i

Hawai'i's first encounter with Europeans occurred in 1778, when Captain James Cook made landfall on the island of Kaua'i. Like the indigenous tribes of North America, the Hawaiians had no immunity to the exotic microbes the Europeans brought with them, and within one century, influenza, smallpox, measles, and syphilis had killed one in two Hawaiians.

So we should keep in mind the background of this public health catastrophe when we judge King Kamehameha's decision to forcibly quarantine his people. It was undeniably cruel. But in the dire circumstances of the moment, it also seemed the prudent thing to do.

Unfortunately, as we understand today, it was also entirely unnecessary. Ninety-five out of every hundred persons are naturally immune to Hansen's disease. And even for those who are susceptible, transmission usually takes prolonged, direct exposure. It was the terrible spectacle of the disease—the skin deformities, the stubby, amputated fingers, the sightlessness—that triggered a reaction far out of proportion to the threat that leprosy actually posed.

The settlement at Kalaupapa was intended to be a self-sufficient farming community, but it did not start out very successfully. Many exiles were seriously ill and in no condition to work. Moreover, the government had not considered the emotional effect of uprooting people and condemning them to a de facto death sentence.

Existential despair combined with the roughness of the living conditions led to an initial period of nihilistic anarchy as a survival-of-the-fittest pecking order was established in the settlement. There was violence and sexual assaults, and new arrivals would be welcomed, not with flowery strings of *leis*, but with a period of brutal hazing.

Gradually, though, a civil society began to form at Kalaupapa. Some of that credit goes to Father Damien de Veuster, a Catholic missionary from Belgium who arrived in 1873. A tireless advocate for the rights and dignity of people with Hansen's disease, Fr. Damien successfully lobbied the government in Honolulu for greater supplies of food and medicine. The lobbyist became a martyr, contracting Hansen's disease and dying of it five years later, in 1889. He was canonized in 2009 and is now St. Damien of Moloka'i.

In the 1940s drugs were finally developed that could treat Hansen's disease. With the threat of new infection virtually eliminated, Kamehameha V's ban was repealed in 1969, and the residents of Kaulalpapa were free to leave. Many, however, chose to stay within the settlement and the only life they had known. In 2003, about forty still remained.

Even after the lifting of the ban, the settlement at Kalaupapa remains closed off from the rest of the world. The sheer wall of the *pali* prevents access to the peninsula by car. There is a small airport, but visitors still typically arrive by foot or mule. In 1980, Kalaupapa was declared a national park, but it is still not exactly a public space. You can visit the old leper colony only at the invitation of a permanent resident or as part of a strictly controlled tour group. You must also be at least sixteen years old.

Go to **www.nps.gov/kala/index.htm** for information on how to visit.

See also:
Syphilitic gummas: Syphilitic brains, Indiana

OK, Cough It Up!

A male frigatebird

WHAT: The Great Frigatebird

WHERE: The Northwestern Hawaiian Islands

It is said that possession is nine-tenths of the law, but this seagoing marauder truly tests the meaning of ownership.

The Great Frigatebird nests among the sea cliffs in a chain of desert islands and atolls that stretch out for hundreds of miles above Kawai'i. Midway—the site of the epic World War II sea battle—is the largest of this leeward batch of Hawaiian islands and about the only one anybody might know by name.

Frigatebirds look like black seagulls, but with disproportionately large wings and a forked tail. Females have white breasts, while the males have a large, obscene, red throat pouch that they inflate during the mating season. The Great Frigatebird's claim to fame, however, is its hunting technique, which is as extraordinary as it is distasteful.

When a hungry frigatebird spies a well-fed seabird, it dashes into hot pursuit. Harassing its mark, the frigatebird will give chase until, nauseated from too much exertion on a full stomach, the other bird vomits up its meal—at which point the wily frigatebird snatches up the disgorged repast and gobbles it down, before it even hits the water.

That neat bit of aerial acrobatics is not gratuitous showboating; it's a necessary survival strategy. Because of its awkwardly large wings, the Great Frigatebird has a hard time taking off from the water. More a glider than a flyer, this bird prefers to get airborne by leaping off cliffs and catching the updraft. Surfing the ocean winds, its great wings become an asset that allows the frigatebird to remain aloft for extended periods with hardly any flapping.

The Great Frigatebird's unusual hunting technique is an example of *kleptoparasitism*, or *thief parasitism*. Kleptoparasitism is not uncommon in the animal world. The vile hyena, of course, makes a career of thieving and scavenging. But even the adorable chinstrap penguin will steal from its neighbor to feather its own nest. And the stately bald eagle, like many other raptor birds, is a bully that will gladly steal prey from weaker hunters.

The stigma of its unsporting survival strategy is reflected in the name of the Great Frigatebird (*Fregata minor*, in the language of science—inexplicably, this means *the lesser frigate*), which derives from *frigate*, a make of old sailing ship that was popular with pirates. Less euphemistically, the Hawaiians simply call this bird *'iwa*, or *thief.*

Grabbing dinner out from under the nose of a clumsy foe is one thing, but retrieving it from someone else's stomach, that really is too much. At the very least, it's a clear violation of the five-second rule.

Alaska

A Parasite That Makes an Ass of Itself

WHAT: Sarcotaces arcticus

WHERE: The southeast coast of Alaska

Fishing in Alaska is big money. Every king crab leg you crack and nearly every morsel of cedar-plank-grilled salmon you savor is fished from Alaskan waters. Almost half the state's private sector jobs are connected to the commercial fishing industry.

Fishing in Alaska is also big danger. Tough work and harsh climate lead to an annual on-the-job death rate that is thirty times the national average—or 124 deaths for every 100,000 workers. This makes fishing in Alaska the most hazardous job in the nation.

Well, it's not easy on the fish either. Eluding human hunters while navigating a gantlet of indigenous subaquatic hazards can be a real pain in the ass.

Sometimes literally, as in the case of *Sarcotaces arcticus*.

This minuscule marine parasite is a member of the *copepod* or *oar-footed* subclass of crustaceans. But *S. arcticus* has traveled so far down its peculiar evolutionary path that it bears almost no resemblance to its armor-clad cousin, the king crab. In fact, it's on the opposite end of the size spectrum. Starting out in life at 3 millimeters, or one-eighth of a good old American inch, *S. arcticus* resembles nothing so closely as a pallid flea with two large paddle feet.

The tiny young *S. arcticus* bobs around the ocean depths, scoping out fish bottoms. When it finds one that catches its fancy—it favors yelloweye, Pacific ocean perch, and other rockfish—*S. arcticus* quickly darts up the anus of its unsuspecting victim, burrows its head into the flesh near the poor fish's rectum, and holds fast. Not content with merely leeching off the ample blood supply of the fish's digestive tract, *S. arcticus* exploits its host in an even more unspeakable way. Diverting its host's own cells, *S. arcticus* uses them to build a protective cyst around itself . . . out of fish anus. The rectal intruder will eventually swell into a two-inch long, teardrop-shaped blob that looks like it has been wrapped in soggy chicken skin.

A youth of enterprise and labor giving way to the morbid obesity of middle age—that is the lot of the female *S. arcticus*, ensconced in her intestinal hideaway. But not so for the male of the species. On the contrary, this parasite of the second order will remain tiny and lithe for the duration of his life, which is lived in utter indolence and indulgence. Never actually building a home of its own, the male *S. arcticus* seeks out an enticingly plump female already anchored securely in a fish's gut and permanently attaches himself to her milky expanse of bloated anus sac, where he will feed off his mate and copulate, more or less without pause.

Not a bad life by any rational standard.

It is very difficult to remove a female *S. arcticus* without rupturing the intestinal wall of her host—which is obviously bad for the fish. It is also likely that in removing *S. arcticus* you'll puncture her sac, causing it to forcefully disgorge its contents of inky-black, semi-digested rockfish blood—which can be upsetting for everyone nearby.

Although it can't imaginably do anything to improve quality of life for its fish-host, *S. arcticus* doesn't seem to harm it in any significant way, either. *S. arcticus* poses no danger to people, aside from the psychological scarring. If you find one in your fish fillet, pull it out and throw it away. And if a little remainder of it sticks, no big deal. As hot dog makers have known for generations, a little extra anus never hurt anyone.

Acknowledgments

No book simply happens all by itself. Indeed, you might be surprised—even dismayed—at how many talented adults colluded to make this one a reality. Several of them deserve special mention.

I would like to thank my editor, Gabrielle Moss, for her unswerving faith in the redeeming social value of this project. Thanks also to Joanna Ebenstein for being the catalyst for letting a thousand stink flowers bloom.

A final thank you to my wife, Jeanine. Not because I have to, but for reals: She's a wickedly tough critic, this darling helpmeet of mine, and not too shabby with a pen, either. Thanks for holding my feet to the flame. You never let me shortchange myself or my readers. In return, you have my word that I will never let your mother see this book.

Like the cheese in the schoolyard rhyme, though, the gross must inevitably stand alone. If anything in these pages has raised your ire or your gorge, O distressed reader, your spleen should be directed at no one but this most chagrined author.

Photo Credits

Page 3: Snap Revell at the 11th Annual Sopchoppy Worm Gruntin' Festival. Photo © 2011 by Nick Baldwin of NBPhotography.

Page 13: A grunion in its natural habitat. Photo by Eric Wittman from Wichita, Kansas, USA. http://www.flickr.com/photos/ricoslounge/21341034/in/photostream/

Page 14: An albino redwood. Photo by Alex Nelson. http://www.flickr.com/photos/loup-vert/3718997373/

Page 23: The Donner Party Statue. Photo by Seano1. http://en.wikipedia.org/wiki/File:Donner_Party_Memorial.jpg

Page 37: The Market Theater Gum Wall. Photo © 2012 by Corinne Manning

Page 46: The Berkeley Pit. Photo by NASA.

Page 51: The Frozen Dead Guy Days parade. Photo © 2012 by Barbara Lawlor.

Page 76: One of Skulls Unlimited's cryptozoology creations—an alien skull. Photo © 2012 by Skulls Unlimited.

Page 83: An example of hair jewelry. Photo by Gabrielle Moss.

Page 93: The corpse flower, beginning to bloom. Photo by Dana Richmond. http://www.flickr.com/photos/danar/223255487/

Page 139: A snot otter salamander Photo by Brian Gratwicke. http://en.wikipedia.org/wiki/File:Hellbender.jpg http://www.flickr.com/photos/19731486@N07/4626787390

Page 152: Two men engaging in the fine art of worm gruntin'. Photo © 2011 by Robert Seidler of Seidler Productions

Page 194: A phrenology chart. Image is public domain.

Page 207: A taxidermied mouse enjoying waffles. Photo © 2011 by Joanna Ebenstein

Page 208: A taxidermied mouse overindulging in spirits. Photo © 2011 by Joanna Ebenstein.

Page 220: An example of a wet specimen—the classic frog in jar. Photo by Gabrielle Moss.

Page 229: The Park Spark Project. Photo © 2010 by Matthew Mazzotta. parksparkproject.com. matthewmazzotta.com

Page 239: View of the Kalaupapa Settlement by Edward Clifford ca. 1880s. http://commons.wikimedia.org/wiki/File:Edward_Clifford_%E2%80%93_View_of_the_Kalaupapa_Settlement3.jpg

Page 245: A male frigatebird. Photo by Aquaimages. http://en.wikipedia.org/wiki/

File:Male_Frigate_bird.jpg

Index

Illustrations are denoted by italic page numbers.

About the Author

Richard Faulk is a freelance writer and editor. A onetime time-travel columnist and occasional education reporter, he has also written about Vikings for Australian tweens, covered academic conferences for Columbia University, and celebrated the films of Pam Grier in *Penthouse*. He lives in the San Francisco Bay Area, where he thinks deeply about trivial matters.

If you enjoyed this book, visit

www.tarcherbooks.com

and sign up for Tarcher's e-newsletter to receive
special offers, giveaway promotions, and
information on hot upcoming releases.

TARCHER
PENGUIN

Great Lives Begin with Great Ideas

New at **www.tarcherbooks.com**
and **www.penguin.com/tarchertalks:**

Tarcher Talks, an online video series featuring
interviews with bestselling authors on everything from creativity and prosperity to 2012
and Freemasonry.

If you would like to place a bulk order
of this book, call 1-800-847-5515.

Printed in the United States
by Baker & Taylor Publisher Services